JAMILA GAVIN

Jamila Gavin was born in Mussoorie, India, in the foothills of the Himalayas, to an Indian father and English mother. The family settled in England where Jamila completed her schooling, was a music student, worked for the BBC and became a mother of two children.

Since her first book, *The Magic Orange Tree,* published in 1979, she has written collections of short stories and several novels. These include *Grandpa Chatterji,* which was shortlisted for the Smarties Award, and *The Surya Trilogy,* of which the first, *The Wheel of Surya*, was runner-up for the Guardian Children's Fiction Award in 1992 and the other two were subsequently shortlisted. *Coram Boy* was published in 2000 and was awarded the Whitbread Children's Book of the Year. Jamila's latest novel, *The Blood Stone*, was published in 2003.

Jamila has also written for television, radio and the stage. Her first original radio play, *The God at the Gate*, was broadcast on Radio 4 in 2001, and shortlisted for the Richard Imison Award. She adapted her children's book, *Monkey in the Stars*, as a play for the Polka Theatre, Wimbledon, and dramatised her book *Grandpa Chatterji* for Channel 4 Schools. In the autumn of 2002, the Polka Theatre produced another of her plays specially commissioned by them, *Just So*, an adaptation of Rudyard Kipling's *Just So Stories*. Jamila has lived in Gloucestershire for over twenty-five years.

HELEN EDMUNDSON

Helen Edmundson's first play, *Flying*, was presented at the National Theatre Studio in 1990. She first came to notice in 1992 with her adaptation of *Anna Karenina* for Shared Experience, for whom she also adapted *The Mill on the Floss* in 1994. Both won awards – the TMA and the Time Out Awards respectively – and both productions were twice revived and extensively toured.

The Clearing was first staged at The Bush Theatre in 1993, winning John Whiting and Time Out Awards, and was revived and toured by Shared Experience, who also staged her adaptation of *War and Peace* at the National Theatre in 1996 and *Gone to Earth* on tour in 2004. *Mother Teresa is Dead* was premiered at the Royal Court Theatre in 2002. Helen lives in West London with her actor husband and their two children.

Other Titles in this Series

CORAM BOY

adapted by

HELEN EDMUNDSON

based on the novel by

JAMILA GAVIN

NICK HERN BOOKS

London

www.nickhernbooks.co.uk

A Nick Hern Book

This stage adaptation of *Coram Boy* first published
in Great Britain as a paperback original in 2005
by Nick Hern Books Limited, 14 Larden Road, London W3 7ST

Coram Boy copyright © 2005 Helen Edmundson
Music copyright © 2005 Adrian Sutton

Helen Edmundson has asserted her right to be identified
as the adapter of this work

Cover image: Peter Holst/Getty Images

Typeset by Country Setting, Kingsdown, Kent CT14 8ES
Printed in Great Britain by Bookmarque, Croydon, Surrey

A CIP catalogue record for this book is available from
the British Library

ISBN-13   978 1 85459 894 3
ISBN-10   1 85459 894 5

Coram Boy was first performed in the Olivier auditorium of the National Theatre, London, on 15 November 2005 (previews from 2 November). The cast was as follows:

Meshak Gardiner	Jack Tarlton
Angel	Justine Mitchell
Dr Smith	Nicholas Tizzard
Thomas Ledbury (as a boy)	Abby Ford
Alexander Ashbrook (as a boy)	Anna Madeley
Otis Gardiner	Paul Ritter
Mrs Lynch	Ruth Gemmell
Miss Price	Inika Leigh Wright
Theodore Claymore	Adam Shipway
Lady Ashbrook	Rebecca Johnson
Isobel Ashbrook	Kelly Williams
Mrs Milcote	Eve Matheson
Melissa, her daughter	Justine Mitchell
Edward Ashbrook	Katherine Manners
Alice Ashbrook	Sophie Bould
Sir William Ashbrook	William Scott-Masson
Alexander (as an adult)	Bertie Carvel
Mrs Hendry	Sharon Maharaj
Toby	Akiya Henry
Aaron	Anna Madeley
Molly	Chetna Pandya
George Frideric Handel	Nicholas Tizzard
Thomas (as an adult)	Stuart McLoughlin
Mr Philip Gaddarn	Paul Ritter

Other parts played by members of the company

Director   Melly Still
Designers   Ti Green and Melly Still
Lighting Designer   Paule Constable
Music and Soundscore   Adrian Sutton
Music Director   Derek Barnes
Choir Management   Jan Winstone
Fight Director   Alison de Burgh
Sound Designer   Christopher Shutt
Dialect Coach   Sally Grace
Company Voice Work   Patsy Rodenburg
Project Development   Tom Morris

Production Note

This play was originally written to be performed on the
National Theatre's Olivier stage; however, there is no reason at
all why it cannot be fully realised in smaller, simpler spaces.
We did make use of the Olivier's revolve and the angel did do
some flying, but other than that, the staging demands were met
by the actors, and by the lighting and the sound. There were no
grand sets, no tricks, no trap doors, no water features. This
open, simple staging is very much what the piece requires.
The scenes, which are often short, need to flow or tumble in
and out of each other – sometimes even overlap – so complicated
set changes may be a hindrance rather than a help. The events
which, on the page, seem particularly difficult to stage –
drowning, flying, babies which move on demand – are really
an invitation for invention. Also, whilst it is sometimes
imperative for the audience to know exactly where a scene is
taking place, it can, at other times, be left safely to the
imagination. For example, I have placed Act Two, Scene
Seventeen, in Mrs Milcote's bedroom, but it does not really
matter where it happens as long as she is alone and the
emotional import of what she says is conveyed.

Helen Edmundson

CORAM BOY

For my parents

Characters

MESHAK GARDINER/MISH
ALEXANDER ASHBROOK
DR SMITH
THOMAS LEDBURY
OTIS GARDINER
MRS LYNCH
MISS PRICE
ANGEL
THEODORE CLAYMORE
LADY ASHBROOK
ISOBEL ASHBROOK
MELISSA MILCOTE
EDWARD ASHBROOK
ALICE ASHBROOK
MRS MILCOTE
SIR WILLIAM ASHBROOK
TOBY GADDARN
AARON DANGERFIELD
MRS HENDRY
MOLLY JENKINS
GEORGE FRIDERIC HANDEL
PHILIP GADDARN

CORAM CHILDREN, GOVERNOR AND STAFF OF
THE CORAM HOSPITAL, MOTHERS, GUESTS,
SERVANTS, BOYS, GIRLS, LADIES, GENTLEMEN,
MUSICIANS, HANGMAN *and others*

*This text went to press before the end of rehearsals and may
differ slightly from the play as performed.*

ACT ONE

Scene One

1742. Gloucester Cathedral. Early evening. Candles flicker in the echoing darkness.

The door creaks open. MESHAK GARDINER, *fourteen, strange-faced, large-limbed, tattered and hungry, enters. He looks about anxiously and listens. At the other end of the nave, the cathedral* CHOIRBOYS *are practising. They are singing an early incarnation of Handel's 'Oh Death, Where Is Thy Sting', which he will eventually rework and use in* Messiah. *The* BOYS *are repeating the same short phrase over and over in response to the* CHOIRMASTER*'s succinct orders. There is no one else about.*

MESHAK (*whispering*). I'm coming, Angel.

> MESHAK *begins his journey down the south aisle. He feels that he shouldn't be in the cathedral, and it takes him all his courage to dare to move forward – past the gargoyles and the bloody crucifixion scenes.*
>
> *A sudden loud burst of playing on the organ sends him scuttling for cover behind a stone pillar, but as soon as it stops he emerges again and continues. He is almost there now. He can see her – his angel. He feels she is calling to him, whispering his name –*'MESHAK'. *She is tucked away in a side-chapel, inconspicuous, but to* MESHAK *she is a beacon – the most beautiful thing he has ever seen or could possibly imagine. He reaches her and stares up at her – this plaster sculpture with long, glowing auburn hair, the bluest eyes and the kindest expression.*

Angel.

> *As he stares, one of the* CHOIRBOYS *begins a solo. The voice is so beautiful, so uplifting. It fills* MESHAK*'s head and heart. Tears start to his eyes. It seems to him like the angel's voice.*

My angel.

> *He reaches his hand up towards her. Then, for one sublime moment, he feels that she is moving, that she has lowered*

her eyes to meet his and that she is smiling upon him. His breath comes more quickly. But the BOY's *singing stops and the moment passes.*

The organ starts up again. MESHAK *sinks to his knees in front of his angel, and gazes up at her as the music washes over him.*

The CHOIR *is clearly visible to us now. The* SOLOIST, *who is standing a little separate from the other* BOYS, *sings the last part of his solo again. This is* ALEXANDER ASHBROOK, *fourteen, intelligent, self-contained, intense. His voice soars up to the rafters.*

Then the other BOYS *join in. But almost immediately, mistakes are made and confusion breaks out. The choirmaster,* DR SMITH, *intervenes.*

DR SMITH. Stop! Stop! Stop!

Gradually the BOYS *stop singing and the organ ceases.*

Lamentable. Is this not the very section we spent half an hour perfecting yesterday?

BOY. It was the new boy, Sir. He threw us out.

There are mutters of agreement from other BOYS.

ALEXANDER. It's the rest in the middle of bar sixteen, Sir. I think some of them . . .

DR SMITH. One moment, Mr Ashbrook. Where is our newcomer?

He scans the CHOIR, *with a stern expression.*

BOYS. Here, Sir. He's here, Sir.

A young open-faced boy, THOMAS LEDBURY, *is nudged and hassled. He puts his hand up.*

THOMAS. Here, Sir.

DR SMITH. Thomas, isn't it?

THOMAS. Yes, Sir. Thomas Ledbury, Sir.

DR SMITH. You can *read* music, Thomas Ledbury?

THOMAS. I'm trying to read the music, Sir. I'll be fine once I've heard the whole tune. Only it's so split up. And it's not very catchy.

The BOYS *snigger.*

DR SMITH. Do you know who wrote this rather sublime anthem?

THOMAS. Mr Handel, I think, Sir.

DR SMITH. George Frideric Handel, the most gifted composer alive today. Would you like me to write to Mr Handel and ask him to send us something more 'catchy'?

Pause. Everyone is looking at THOMAS.

THOMAS. More catchy?

Pause.

Well, yes please, Sir. That would certainly help.

The BOYS *burst out laughing.*

DR SMITH. Enough! Enough! We will finish there for today. Work at it. Learn it.

Evening chores, boys!

The BOYS *let out a groan as they begin to move off, but there is a lot of chattering and laughing too.* THOMAS *is pushed out with them.* ALEXANDER *approaches* DR SMITH, *who is hurriedly sorting out his music and about to leave.*

ALEXANDER. Dr Smith?

DR SMITH. Mr Ashbrook. Nil desperandum. We shall make silk purses of them yet.

ALEXANDER. Can I talk to you in confidence, Sir?

DR SMITH. Of course, of course. Come to my study in half an hour.

ALEXANDER. I want to stay on. At the cathedral.

DR SMITH *stops and gives him his full attention.*

I want to stay on, after my voice . . . after it . . .

DR SMITH. Breaks?

ALEXANDER. Yes, Sir.

DR SMITH. Hum. I suppose it can't be long now. You have turned fourteen, have you not?

ALEXANDER. I'm almost fifteen. I have to carry on with my music, Sir. Even if my voice . . . even if I can't sing in the choir, I have to go on with my playing and I have to go on studying Handel with you. Please, Sir, would you write to my father and ask him if I can stay? Tell him how well I'm doing and how important my music is.

DR SMITH. This is very difficult.

ALEXANDER. I think he would take notice if you wrote to him.

DR SMITH. You are undoubtedly extremely gifted, Alexander. Your voice is the best treble Gloucester has heard in many a long year, and your understanding of music is exceptional . . .

ALEXANDER. Music is my life.

DR SMITH. But I'm sure your father plans higher things for you.

ALEXANDER. There is nothing higher than music.

DR SMITH. Indeed. You and I know that, but does he? As for him taking notice of me, I very much doubt that he would. It's not my place to interfere in these matters.

ALEXANDER. Please, Sir. You're my only hope.

DR SMITH *considers the situation.*

DR SMITH. Well, well. I can see no harm in writing to him and suggesting you might be allowed to stay.

ALEXANDER. Thank you, Sir!

DR SMITH. Suggesting, mind. And you must discuss it with him at Easter.

ALEXANDER. Yes, Sir. I will, Sir.

DR SMITH. Good boy. Good boy. Nil desperandum.

DR SMITH *leaves.* ALEXANDER *is filled with hope. He kneels down and prays.*

ALEXANDER. Please. Please . . .

MESHAK, *thinking he is alone, stands up in front of his angel. He sings a phrase he remembers from* ALEXANDER*'s solo – the phrase which brought his angel to life. His voice is strange and rough, but the notes are recognisable.*

ALEXANDER *hears and goes towards the voice. He sees*
MESHAK *staring up at his angel, singing. He watches him*
for a moment before answering one of MESHAK's *phrases,*
by singing a phrase himself.

MESHAK *looks round, terrified at having been caught.*
ALEXANDER *stares at him. For a moment there is a*   ✓   19
strange sense of sameness and recognition between them.

Who are you?

But at this moment, DR SMITH *comes back in to collect*
something. He sees MESHAK *and comes towards him,*
flapping his arms.

DR SMITH. Out! Out, out! This is not a shelter for vagrants!
Out with you!

MESHAK *charges past* ALEXANDER *and out.*

Scene Two

MESHAK *finds himself on the crowded streets of Gloucester.*
Everyone is hurrying. A bell is ringing. He looks about
desperately.

MESHAK. Da? (*Shouting.*) Da?

He sees a familiar face.

Where's my Da?

WOMAN. He went to catch the ferry. He was looking for you,
Meshak!

MESHAK *looks horrified and immediately runs off.*

Scene Three

On the banks of the River Severn. A crowd of people – many
with carts or livestock – have formed a disorderly queue to
wait for the ferry. Overhead, seagulls cry. The sun is sinking
low in the sky. In the middle of the queue is a covered wagon,
with a horse at the front. Behind the wagon three mules are
tethered, one behind the other. Across the mules' backs there
are heavy-looking saddle-bags. The mules are waiting

*patiently, heads down, munching the grass. In front of the
wagon stands its owner – OTIS GARDINER – dark-haired, in
the prime of his life, he exudes charm and confidence. He has
spread a white sail-cloth on the ground and on it he displays
the pots and pans and tools which are his wares. A small
crowd has gathered to look and buy. OTIS completes a sale
and jumps up on the wagon.*

OTIS. Last chance! Last chance now for your pots and ladles,
buckets, string, ribbons, thread, all your household needs!
Last chance now! The ferry's on its way! Grab it while you
can, now!

Two GIRLS pass by.

GIRL 1. I can see something I wouldn't mind grabbing.

The other GIRL laughs.

OTIS. Knives sharpened!

They pick up some ribbons. OTIS homes in on them.

Like the ribbons, do you, girls?

GIRL 2. She likes everything you've got.

OTIS. Glad to hear it. I aim to please.

GIRL 2. I bet you do.

OTIS hands them each a ribbon.

OTIS. Let's see now – Rose White . . . and Rose Red.

The GIRLS giggle.

Tuppence each.

GIRL 1. That's more than they are on Gloucester market.

OTIS. I don't buy cheap, I don't sell cheap. Quality costs.

*MESHAK hurtles up, panting and pale. OTIS shoots him a
glance but carries on with the sale – taking money from the
GIRLS. He winks at them.*

You be sure to tie 'em tight. They're easily undone.

*They laugh and go on their way. A bell is ringing now,
announcing that the ferry is in and there is a surge of
activity as PEOPLE prepare to board. OTIS corners
MESHAK when no one is looking.*

Where the hell were you?

MESHAK. Sorry, Da . . .

OTIS. I've got the biggest meeting of my life tonight and you could have made me miss it. Why do you always, always, always hold me back, eh?

MESHAK. I'm sorry, Da.

OTIS. You just thank your lucky stars that ferry was late. Now start packing up. And check the saddle-bags, one of 'em's loose.

MESHAK *does as he was told.*

(*Shouting out.*) That's it now! That's it! If you want it, now's the time!

A MAN *approaches the wagon with three bedraggled* CHILDREN *trailing behind him.*

MAN. Otis Gardiner?

OTIS *glances up but then goes on with what he's doing.*

Can you take these children? I'll give you a shilling for each one.

OTIS. Can't do it. I've got four in the wagon already.

MAN. And you're worried about overcrowding, I suppose?

OTIS. What I'm worried about is getting to The Black Dog in Frampton by nine o'clock. What I'm worried about is my wagon getting stuck in mud because it's overloaded with brats.

MAN. I've walked two miles to find you. I was told you were reliable.

OTIS. When I want to be.

MAN. I'll pay over the odds.

OTIS *glances at the* CHILDREN.

OTIS. Well now . . . There's a wool mill at Downham that asked for four; I reckon I could get 'em to take six. And I know of a farm or two wanting boys.

MAN. They're strong, look – healthy.

OTIS. I want five shillings for each one I take.

MAN. You're jesting, man! That's robbery!

OTIS. It'd cost you a lot more than that to keep them in your workhouse for the next five years, and you know it. Five shillings. Take it or leave it.

The bell on the ferry rings again.

(*Shouting out.*) That's it! We're moving!

MAN. I'll take it.

OTIS. Meshak!

MESHAK *runs to him.*

In with the others.

MESHAK *takes the eldest* BOY's *arm and leads him to the wagon. The others follow, shaking and wretched.* MESHAK *pushes each one inside.*

As OTIS *completes the transaction with the* MAN, MESHAK *goes back to checking the saddle-bags. As he starts to tighten the buckle on one, it falls open slightly and a small arm – what looks like a baby's arm – reaches out into the air.* MESHAK *stares at it for a moment, then hurriedly pushes it back into the bag and fastens the bag up tight.*

The MAN *leaves. The* PEOPLE *in front are moving forward.* OTIS *jumps up onto the wagon.*

Get up here, Meshak! We're on the move!

Scene Four

In the schoolroom at the cathedral, THOMAS *has been blindfolded and tied up with a rope by some of the other* BOYS. *They are spinning him round and round and then laughing as they let go of him and watch him stagger about.*

BOY. Wait, wait!

The other BOYS *stand very still. The* BOY *approaches* THOMAS.

THOMAS. Are you there? Who's that? Can we stop this now? I . . .

But the BOY *shoves an apple into* THOMAS's *mouth so that he can't speak. All the* BOYS *laugh uproariously. They spin him again.*

ALEXANDER *enters and takes in the situation, watching for a moment or two. Then:*

ALEXANDER. Let him go.

The BOYS *stop laughing and look round at him.*

BOY. Why should we?

There is a moment of tension.

BOY 2. May as well. We were going to let him go soon anyway.

BOY 3. We all had it done to us.

ALEXANDER. I know that. But I think he's had enough now.

There is another tense moment as the BOYS *wait for their leader's decision.*

BOY. Looks like the little gentleman has spoken. Come on, boys.

The BOYS *traipse out. When they have gone,* ALEXANDER *goes to* THOMAS. *He removes the blindfold and takes the apple out of his mouth.*

THOMAS. Thank you very much. I was starting to feel a bit sick there.

ALEXANDER *unties the rope.*

Thank you. Thank you very much.

ALEXANDER. You don't have to thank me. If they'd caught a rat and spun it round by the tail, I'd have done the same.

THOMAS. Still.

He sees that ALEXANDER *is about to throw the apple away.*

Oh, I'll have it if you don't mind.

ALEXANDER *hands him the apple.*

Thank you very much. Are you the best fighter then? You must be. My Da said, find out who the best fighter is and stick to him like a limpet.

ALEXANDER. I don't fight. They do what I say because my father is the richest and my voice is the best. They're scared of what would happen if they touched me.

THOMAS. Still. I'm very grateful. I know it's just a bit of fun, but yesterday they stuck my head in a piss-pot, and the day before that they took me up the tower blindfold and made me walk out onto the parapet. I'm scared of heights. Are you scared of anything?

ALEXANDER. Wasting time.

ALEXANDER *starts to leave.*

THOMAS. Wait.

THOMAS *makes a flamboyant bow to* ALEXANDER.

Thomas Ledbury.

ALEXANDER *bows reluctantly.*

ALEXANDER. Alexander Ashbrook.

THOMAS. I owe you my life, Sir!

ALEXANDER. Forget it. You owe me nothing.

ALEXANDER *leaves.*

Scene Five

The dingy upstairs of The Black Dog in the Gloucestershire countryside. It is late evening. The sounds of a rowdy night drift up from downstairs. A woman, MRS LYNCH, *is standing outside one of the bedrooms with a candle in her hand. She is plainly dressed, with strong features and an unchanging, inscrutable expression.*

OTIS *comes along the corridor, with* MESHAK *following behind him.*

MRS LYNCH. Where have you been?

OTIS. Where is she?

MRS LYNCH. In there. She wouldn't walk through the door downstairs, I had to bring her up the back way.

OTIS (*smoothing his hair*). How do I look?

MRS LYNCH *takes a comb from her pocket and hands it to him. He combs his hair.*

MRS LYNCH. It's been all I can do to make her wait.

OTIS. I knew you'd think of something. You always do.

MRS LYNCH. Hello, Meshak.

MESHAK. Hello.

MRS LYNCH. He's grown. He looks almost a man.

OTIS. He's grown but his brain hasn't.

MRS LYNCH. He should stay back until he's needed.

OTIS. He knows what to do – don't you, boy?

MESHAK. Yes, Da.

OTIS. Right, let's get in there, shall we?

MRS LYNCH. If you're ready?

OTIS. Oh, I'm ready.

> *They enter the room. Inside, it is almost dark. There is a small bed and on it there is a Moses basket covered with a white shawl. At the far end of the room, a very young lady, MISS PRICE, is standing. She seems to take fright when they come in and she clings to the wall for support. MESHAK stays in the darkness by the door. There is silence for several moments.*

MISS PRICE. Is this him?

MRS LYNCH. Yes.

OTIS. Good evening, Miss. I'm sorry to have kept you waiting.

MISS PRICE. Are you the Coram Man?

> OTIS *glances at* MRS LYNCH.

MRS LYNCH. Yes. The Coram Man.

MISS PRICE. Oh, God forgive me. God forgive me.

> MESHAK *moves, disturbed by her distress.*

Who's that?

OTIS. My boy, Miss.

MRS LYNCH. He's harmless.

OTIS. He's gentle and sweet as a lamb, though he don't look it.

> MISS PRICE *is almost collapsing with anxiety and fear.*

MRS LYNCH. You should sit down.

MISS PRICE *doesn't respond.*

OTIS. Mrs Lynch here tells me you have a little 'un as needs looking after.

Pause. OTIS *begins to wonder if she heard him.*

MISS PRICE. Tell me, please . . . tell me about Thomas Coram.

OTIS. Thomas Coram? Oh, he's a kind and gentle man, Miss. As good as they come. The next time they're making saints, I reckon he'll be up there. He was a sea captain, and he went to the New World and built ships. And when he came back he was so shocked, so appalled – I think that was the word he used – by seeing all the orphans and the little babies abandoned on the streets of London, that he set up his hospital for foundling children.

MISS PRICE. You have met him?

OTIS. Only once, Miss. He tipped his hat to me and shook me by the hand. And I felt a warm glow all over. And when I'd sat down and recovered myself, I thought, 'That was the goodness – that was the goodness pouring from him.'

MISS PRICE. Yes.

OTIS. And it's a very grand place, Miss, the Foundling Hospital, all new and clean and with fields all around for the little 'uns to play in and big gates at the front to keep out trouble. And the little 'uns eat good food and wear fine uniforms . . .

MISS PRICE. And the babies . . . I have heard that the babies are properly nursed?

OTIS *looks at* MRS LYNCH. *He doesn't know the answer to this.*

MRS LYNCH. The babies go to the country to be nursed and weaned.

OTIS. By the kindest of women. Women who know about babies.

MRS LYNCH. Then when they're old enough, they are taken to live at the hospital.

OTIS. They get taught to read and write and get apprenticed to the most respectable folk. I promise you, Miss, your little fellow couldn't get a better start in this world.

MISS PRICE. It's a girl. My baby is a girl.

OTIS. Oh, I'm sorry. I always assume they're boys with having a boy myself, you see.

MESHAK, *who has been listening intently to this description of a wonderful, safe place, recognises his cue just in time and goes to his father.* OTIS *strokes his head and pets him.*

His poor dear mother was taken by the angels. There's only me to care for him. But we do all right, don't we, son?

MESHAK. Yes, Da. Thank you, Da.

OTIS *waits a moment, then steps towards the basket.*

OTIS. Here, is she?

MISS PRICE (*aggressively*). Don't!

OTIS *freezes.*

I mean . . . please don't. Mercy. Her name is Mercy.

There is a long pause.

MRS LYNCH. Can you be sure that Coram will take the child?

OTIS. Oh yes, they'll take her from me. All I need is the money for my services and then a little more from time to time to pass on to the hospital, so as they can keep her in the best. Paper and pens and fancy cakes on her birthdays . . .

MISS PRICE. Her birthdays . . .

She fights back the tears which threaten to overwhelm her.

MRS LYNCH. You knew this would be difficult. You must remember what we said.

MISS PRICE. I can't . . . I can't do this.

MRS LYNCH. What is the choice? Tell me?

OTIS. Now wait a minute. If the young lady doesn't want to give me her baby then she shouldn't. The Coram Hospital can't take many and there are other babies I could take instead.

MISS PRICE. No, wait. Wait. Wait a moment, would you please? Please.

MESHAK (*suddenly*). Birthdays.

She stands for several moments, struggling with herself.
Then she moves towards the bed.

MISS PRICE. There is a bag here . . . with clean linen for
when she has grown a little. And a letter, explaining . . . It
can't be right . . .

She breaks off and tries again to control herself.

There's a ring on a ribbon around her neck. It was my
mother's.

OTIS. I understand, Miss.

MISS PRICE (*quietly*). Take her.

OTIS. What was that, Miss?

She takes out a silk purse full of money and hands it to him.

MISS PRICE. Take her.

OTIS *takes the purse and nods.* MRS LYNCH *goes to the*
bed and picks up the bag.

And you will come to me and tell me how she is?

OTIS. Yes, Miss.

She stares at the basket and is about to lift the shawl.

MRS LYNCH. No. Remember what we said.

MISS PRICE *takes her hand from the basket.* OTIS *steps*
forward and is about to pick it up, but MISS PRICE
clutches his hand.

MISS PRICE. Look me in the eye.

He does so.

Swear to me, on your son's life, that you will take my
daughter to Thomas Coram and she will be cared for.

OTIS. On my son's life, I swear it.

Scene Six

In the cathedral, THOMAS *is standing on a chair singing 'The*
Gloucester Clipper'. There is a group of BOYS *gathered*
around him, laughing and clapping. ALEXANDER *enters,*
carrying a violin and some music. He watches and listens.

THOMAS.
>At Gloucester docks, so I heard tell,
>Where fisherwives gather, their catch to sell,
>The rarest vessel you ever did see,
>Cries, who will come fishing, come fishing with me.

Chorus.

>Over and under and haul him to sea,
>Who will come fishing, come fishing with me.

>I'm a fast-going clipper, kind fellows, cried she,
>I'm ready for cargo, my hold it is free,
>Come give me a rope now and take me in tow,
>From yardarm to yardarm a-towing we'll go.

Chorus.

>Billy stepped up, he was ready to go,
>He clambered aboard and she took him below,
>He lifted her hatches, found plenty of space,
>But his jib-boom was bent and he sank without trace.

Chorus.

>Johnny was desperate and up for the chase,
>He drew alongside at a hell of a pace,
>Her foresails were lowered, her staysails undone,
>But his shot-locker emptied before he'd begun.

Chorus.

>Her eye fell on Thomas, so handsome and fine,
>Her prow rose to meet him, she threw him a line,
>He filled her with fishes, she begged him for more,
>And he never let up 'til he'd run her ashore.

Chorus.

>Here's luck to the girl with the curly black locks,
>Here's luck to the girl who ran Bill on the rocks,
>Here's luck to the girl who led Johnny astray,
>Raise a cheer now for Thomas who showed her the way.

Chorus.

The BOYS *cheer and* THOMAS *bows, delighted to have been such a success. The* BOYS *run off.* THOMAS *sees* ALEXANDER.

THOMAS. Robbie Keck's finest. He's a sailor who comes in The Anchor. He taught me all the songs I know. He'd teach me a song and then I'd get up on a table and sing it, and everyone would clap, and some of them would throw coins for me. You'd be surprised how much I'd get. And then one day this man came in and said to my Da that I'd got a voice, and that he should send me to the cathedral for a scholarship. And here I am.

ALEXANDER. Yes, here you are; singing lewd songs and defiling the house of God. Singing songs like that in here is sacrilegious.

THOMAS (*aghast*). Oh. Still. It's stopped them picking on me; God might be glad about that, don't you think?

ALEXANDER *comes towards him.*

ALEXANDER. Dr Smith says you play the violin.

THOMAS. The violin? Yes, yes I do.

ALEXANDER. There's a part in this piece for a violin. Perhaps you could play it through for me.

THOMAS. Course! I'll do it with pleasure.

He takes the violin from ALEXANDER. *He looks at the music and his face falls.*

Oh. Well . . . I mean, I'll give it a try.

ALEXANDER. You don't have to.

THOMAS. No, no. I will.

THOMAS *begins to play but quickly falters.*

Oh, that's a sharp, is it? Sorry, I . . .

He tries again.

Oops . . . that's that sharp again, isn't it?

ALEXANDER. Let's leave it.

THOMAS. No, please. Sing it for me. What I have to play. Please.

ALEXANDER *sings through the music, reluctantly. As soon as he has finished,* THOMAS *plays it back to him on the violin.* ALEXANDER *stares at him in amazement.*

Sorry. Did I get a note wrong?

ALEXANDER. No. No you didn't. You played it perfectly. Can you do it again?

THOMAS. Course.

He does so. ALEXANDER *just stares and stares.*

I've always been able to do that. I only have to hear 7
something once and I can play it.

ALEXANDER. So can I.

THOMAS. Really?

ALEXANDER. But I've never met anyone else who can do it.

THOMAS. Neither have I.

They smile at each other like long-lost brothers.

ALEXANDER. And do you hear music in your head, all the
time?

THOMAS. Yes, I suppose I do. I always have a song going
round in my head.

ALEXANDER. And do you see colours? When you hear
different notes? Reds and blinding whites and violets?

THOMAS. Not really. But I'd like to, I really would!

ALEXANDER. When I hear a piece of Handel, I see colours
like . . . like fireworks exploding in my head. And sometimes
they're like rivers of colours – soft rivers of yellow or amber
or grey.

THOMAS. That's amazing.

ALEXANDER. Dr Smith says it's a gift.

THOMAS. A gift from who?

ALEXANDER. From God.

THOMAS. Lawks. Is this Handel? Did you see colours then?

ALEXANDER. This isn't Handel.

THOMAS. Shame. But did you see colours?

ALEXANDER. Actually . . . it's mine.

THOMAS. What do you mean? You don't mean you wrote it?

ALEXANDER. I did.

THOMAS. You wrote it? But it's beautiful.

ALEXANDER *smiles bashfully.*

ALEXANDER. I was lying in bed, playing through some Handel in my head and seeing the colours, and then different music started to come, and I started to put the colours together in different ways and I realised it was my music. It was coming from me.

THOMAS *is just staring at him.*

THOMAS. I don't know what to say.

ALEXANDER. So now I'm trying to write it all down.

THOMAS. You really have got a gift.

ALEXANDER. Well, so have you.

THOMAS. No. I can just pick up a tune.

ALEXANDER. You have. You're gifted, Thomas.

They look at each other in awe.

Promise me you'll never waste time singing those silly songs again.

THOMAS. What, never?

ALEXANDER. From now on you've got to work at your music. We'll both work. We'll work together.

Scene Seven

By a dark lake on the Ashbrook estate. Night. OTIS *and* MESHAK *ride up with their wagon and mules.* OTIS *brings the horse to a stop and jumps down. He looks about and listens. There is no human sound.* MESHAK *gets down too.* OTIS *takes a spade from the back of the wagon and thrusts it at him. He points at a patch of muddy ground.*

OTIS. Over there.

MESHAK takes the spade and starts to dig a series of small holes. OTIS *calls into the wagon.*

Get out here.

There are three CHILDREN *remaining now. They come out, looking terrified and cold.*

Go over there and do your business, then stay there until I call you. And don't think of running off – there's wolves in this wood as big as lions.

The CHILDREN *scuttle into the cover of the trees.* OTIS *goes to the saddle-bags and starts to undo them. He looks round at* MESHAK.

Get on with it.

MESHAK *finishes digging and comes to him. They are well hidden from the* CHILDREN *by the wagon.* OTIS *reaches into the first saddle-bag and pulls out a tiny baby. It's not moving. He tosses it at* MESHAK *who takes it and drops it in one of the holes. Then he covers it with earth.*

This is repeated three times. Then OTIS *pulls the final baby from a bag. This one is moving – strong, distinct kicks and stretches. He hands it to* MESHAK.

MESHAK. Still alive.

OTIS. Never mind about that. Wait!

OTIS *takes a ring on a ribbon from around the baby's neck.*

Waste not want not. Now, drop it in.

MESHAK *carries the baby to the last hole in the mud. He stands for a moment, unable to bring himself to bury her. The baby – Mercy – makes a small gurgling sound. He quickly squats and drops her into the hole. He grabs the spade and begins to cover her with earth. Her arms and legs are still moving. He starts to retch but forces himself to go on, all his instincts, his whole being in rebellion against himself. She is gone. He drops the spade and goes to vomit against a tree.*

OTIS *picks up the spade and looks down at the grave.*

Bye bye, Mercy. Thanks for everything.

He goes to get the CHILDREN.

MESHAK *sinks down onto his knees, then sprawls flat on the ground. His eyeballs roll back in his head and his hands twitch. We are plunged into the strange, suspended world of* MESHAK's *'dead' state. It is almost like being underwater – we can hear the sound of his blood rushing and banging in his ears. Distorted distant voices and memories rear up and fade away. Then the babies seem to rise up from the earth and the sound of their mothers' cries fill his head.*

MESHAK. Angel! Angel!

A distant light appears – gorgeous and benign, full of the promise of release and joy. And from the light comes his ANGEL. She is smiling at him – reaching out to him. But she is still distant.

Angel? Angel, take me with you.

ANGEL. Not yet, Meshak. Not yet.

OTIS, *having got the* CHILDREN *back in the wagon, comes over to* MESHAK *and sees him lying on the ground in his 'dead' state.* OTIS *kicks him.*

OTIS. For God's sake, don't start that idiot nonsense now. Get up!

He kicks him again and again.

God damn you!

He picks MESHAK *up and throws him into the back of the wagon. Then he gets up in front and drives off. Only the babies in the ground are left.*

Scene Eight

In the cathedral, the BOYS *are singing 'Oh Death, Where Is Thy Sting'.* DR SMITH *is smiling as he conducts.* ALEXANDER *sings his solo, his voice cutting through the air.* THOMAS *is standing beside him, gazing up in admiration. Then, just for a moment,* ALEXANDER*'s voice falters – cracks slightly – but then it is back. The rest of the* CHOIR *join in and the song comes to an end triumphantly. There is silence for a few moments.*

DR SMITH. Yes. Yes. Yes. Remember it, boys. Hold it in your hearts.

The cathedral clock chimes. All the BOYS *break into a spontaneous cheer.*

Happy Easter!

Some of them call back to him:

BOYS. Thank you, Sir! And you, Sir!

The BOYS *begin to run off to collect their things and head home.* ALEXANDER *turns to* THOMAS, *smiling.*

ALEXANDER. Are you ready?

THOMAS. Course.

DR SMITH *calls out as he leaves:*

DR SMITH. Talk to your father, Mr Ashbrook!

ALEXANDER. Yes, Sir. I will! (*To* THOMAS.) Come on.
Let's go and get our things.

THOMAS *holds up a very small bag he is carrying.*

THOMAS. This *is* my things.

ALEXANDER. Oh. Well, come and help me with mine.

They start to head off.

THOMAS. Is it a very long walk to your house?

ALEXANDER. We're not walking. They're sending the
carriage.

Scene Nine

*The drawing room at Ashbrook House – a grand and sumptuously
furnished room with large, high windows.* LADY ASHBROOK,
*elegant and confident, is in the middle of a meeting with the
local magistrate,* MR THEODORE CLAYMORE.

CLAYMORE. I do understand, Lady Ashbrook, that the
foundation of an orphanage on the Ashbrook estate is a
project close to your heart.

LADY ASHBROOK. Next to my family, it is my chief concern.

CLAYMORE. But I must warn you that the parish officers are
very much opposed to the scheme.

LADY ASHBROOK. Then I will have to overcome their
objections. In this day and age, it is simply not acceptable
for us to turn our backs on the needs of destitute children.
The late Queen herself threw her support behind the
foundation of the new Foundling Hospital in London.

CLAYMORE. The Coram Hospital – I have heard of it.

LADY ASHBROOK. If that is not enough to make us recognise
our moral responsibility then I don't know what is.

CLAYMORE. The fact of the matter, My Lady, is that an orphanage here at Ashbrook will draw desperate women from miles around. They will cross into our parish to give birth simply because they know their infants will be well supported here.

LADY ASHBROOK. And that is something we should fear?

CLAYMORE. There are a great many other demands on parish funds. I believe the church is in need of new pews. And the upkeep of the almshouses is costing a great deal more than anticipated . . .

A girl – ISOBEL – suddenly bursts into the room. She is thirteen years old, pretty and animated. She is shortly followed by another girl – older and extremely lovely, with golden hair and piercing blue eyes. This is MELISSA.

ISOBEL. Mama, it's Alex! He's here! (*Realising she is interrupting.*) Sorry.

LADY ASHBROOK. Isobel, this is Mr Claymore, the magistrate. Isobel – my eldest daughter.

CLAYMORE. Charming. Quite charming. And who is this young lady?

LADY ASHBROOK. Melissa Milcote – my cousin's girl.

CLAYMORE. And how old are you, Miss Milcote?

MELISSA. Fifteen, Sir.

CLAYMORE. Fifteen. Then I predict we will soon be witnessing an outbreak of lovesick young men.

ISOBEL *smiles but* MELISSA *only looks down.*

If all children were to turn out so well, Lady Ashbrook, the parish might welcome them with open arms.

LADY ASHBROOK. Perhaps all children would, Mr Claymore, if they were given the chance.

ISOBEL. Do hurry, Mama. His carriage is almost at the door.

ISOBEL *bobs a curtsy to* MR CLAYMORE *and runs out.* MELISSA *follows her.*

LADY ASHBROOK. My son is returning from school.

CLAYMORE. Then I will not detain you any longer. My Lady, I have sat as a Justice for some years. I know the lower

OLIVIER THEATRE

CORAM BOY

MON 9 JAN 2006 7:30 PM

COGR   AISLE 2

£15.00   **D41**

CHEQUE   CIRCLE   ON LEVEL 3

The National Theatre presents an eclectic mix of new plays and classics, with seven or eight productions in repertory at any one time. Through an extensive programme of talks and readings, backstage tours, free foyer music, exhibitions and outdoor entertainment the National recognises that theatre doesn't begin and end with the rise and fall of the curtain. Come along early to enjoy a Platform performance, free live music, exhibitions, a meal or a drink. For full details visit www.nationaltheatre.org.uk or see our current leaflet.

Foyers open Monday to Saturday, 10am–11pm
(opening hours on public holidays may vary)

Box Office 020 7452 3000
Information 020 7452 3400
Minicom 020 7452 3009
Groups (10+) 020 7452 3010

24hr booking online
www.nationaltheatre.org.uk

orders better than most. It is my considered opinion that anything which encourages wanton procreation or the begetting of illegitimate children is doing them, and society as a whole, no favours whatsoever. I only ask that you consider what I have said.

Scene Ten

ALEXANDER *and* THOMAS *have arrived in front of the wide, golden-stone steps of Ashbrook House.* THOMAS *is standing very still, utterly shocked by the size of the house.* ISOBEL *rushes from inside and throws her arms around* ALEXANDER.

MRS MILCOTE, *an anxious middle-aged lady, appears on the steps with* MELISSA. *Two little children –* EDWARD *and* ALICE *– run past them to reach* ALEXANDER.

ISOBEL. Alex! Is it really you?

ALEXANDER. Hello, Issy.

EDWARD *and* ALICE. Alex! Alex!

ALEXANDER. Hello, little people.

ALICE. Are you staying forever?

ALEXANDER. Two weeks.

EDWARD *and* ALICE *are wild with excitement.*

EDWARD *and* ALICE. Two weeks! Two weeks!

MRS MILCOTE. Edward! Alice! Control yourselves.

EDWARD. How long is two weeks?

ALEXANDER. Well, I suppose it's like forever to you.

ISOBEL (*beckoning him*). Come. Come, come. Alex, this is Mrs Milcote. She has come to be our governess. She's Mama's cousin, you know?

ALEXANDER. Pleased to meet you, Ma'am.

MRS MILCOTE. We have heard so much about you, Alexander. Melissa and I have been longing to meet you. My daughter, Melissa.

ALEXANDER. How do you do?

MELISSA. How do you do?

ALEXANDER. And this is my good friend Thomas Ledbury. Come here, Thomas.

THOMAS *approaches shyly.*

ISOBEL. It's lovely to meet you, Thomas. I'm Isobel.

THOMAS. Lovely to meet you, Miss. (*To* MRS MILCOTE.) And you, Mrs Ashbrook.

ALEXANDER. This isn't my mother, Thomas.

MRS MILCOTE. Here is *Lady* Ashbrook now.

LADY ASHBROOK *sweeps up and kisses* ALEXANDER.

LADY ASHBROOK. Alex. Darling boy.

ALEXANDER. Hello, Mama.

LADY ASHBROOK. And this must be your friend Thomas. Welcome to Ashbrook House, Thomas.

THOMAS. Thank you very much.

LADY ASHBROOK. You must make yourself entirely at home.

EDWARD (*looking at* THOMAS). Why is he wearing those funny clothes?

ALEXANDER. That's our uniform.

LADY ASHBROOK. And how was your journey?

ALEXANDER. Fine.

THOMAS. It was the best! We came in a carriage!

LADY ASHBROOK. Really? And you've brought the sunshine with you.

THOMAS. That's what I said!

MRS LYNCH *has appeared on the steps behind them.*

LADY ASHBROOK. Mrs Lynch?

MRS LYNCH *comes to her.*

12

Thomas, this is Mrs Lynch, our housekeeper. Anything you need, you must let her know. Which bedroom have you put Thomas in?

MRS LYNCH. The yellow room, My Lady.

LADY ASHBROOK. Excellent. The yellow room is perfect for such a sunny boy. Kindly show him where it is.

EDWARD *and* ALICE. We'll show him! We'll show him!

They grab hold of THOMAS *and pull him to the house.*

LADY ASHBROOK. That's right, children. Careful now!

ISOBEL. Poor Thomas.

LADY ASHBROOK. What a sweet boy.

ALEXANDER. He's a very talented violinist. He's been helping me with my music.

LADY ASHBROOK. Do you think it's possible that those are his only decent clothes?

ALEXANDER. Probably.

LADY ASHBROOK. Then we must unearth some of your old ones. I'm sure we have plenty to fit him. Perhaps you could help me to organise that, Margaret?

MRS MILCOTE. Certainly.

LADY ASHBROOK. We shall all dine together today, darling. A special treat because you're home.

ALEXANDER. Thank you, Mama.

LADY ASHBROOK. Cook has made all your favourites. Half an hour everyone.

LADY ASHBROOK *and* MRS MILCOTE *leave.*

There is an awkward pause. MELISSA *gets the impression that* ALEXANDER *wishes her to go.*

MELISSA. I'll leave you two alone.

ISOBEL. Oh, don't. She doesn't have to, does she, Alex?

ALEXANDER *doesn't reply quickly enough.*

MELISSA. You must have a lot to talk about.

MELISSA *leaves.*

ISOBEL. Isn't she beautiful? Don't you think she's so beautiful?

ALEXANDER. I'm afraid I don't notice things like that.

ISOBEL. Well, you should. And she is. And I'm so relieved that she's come. I was dying of boredom without you and now she and I have become the best of friends.

ALEXANDER. Is Papa here, Issy?

ISOBEL. He's in Bristol. One of his ships is due back.

ALEXANDER. You haven't heard him talking about a letter, have you? About a letter from Dr Smith?

ISOBEL. No. But he'll have to be back before Saturday, because you'll never guess what. (ALEXANDER *doesn't respond.*) Guess what!

ALEXANDER. Sorry. What?

ISOBEL. We're giving a ball on Saturday for Mama's birthday. And I'm allowed to stay up for it. Right until the end. My first ball. Isn't it wonderful?

ALEXANDER. It's wonderful if you think it's wonderful.

She hugs him.

Scene Eleven

A sunny day. The ASHBROOK SIBLINGS *and* THOMAS *arrive before an idyllic-looking cottage in a corner of the grounds. There is a duck pond in front of it with a little bridge across, leading to the front door. The sound of music can be heard coming from within.* THOMAS *is wearing a blindfold.* EDWARD *has hold of one of his arms, and* ALICE *the other.*

EDWARD. Just a little further now.

ALICE. No peeping, Thomas.

THOMAS. We're not anywhere high, are we?

ALEXANDER. No. We wouldn't do that to you.

They get him into position, facing the cottage. ISOBEL *removes the blindfold.*

ISOBEL. Now . . . open your eyes!

He does so, and his face lights up.

THOMAS. Oh!

ALICE. It's our house.

ISOBEL. It's called Waterside.

THOMAS. Waterside.

EDWARD. No grown-ups allowed.

THOMAS. Really?

ISOBEL. Only Nanny sometimes.

EDWARD. And Mama comes for tea.

ALICE. Only when we say.

THOMAS. It's wonderful. It's like a house in a story, hidden away in the trees and with the pond and the ducks and everything.

ISOBEL. And it's perfect inside. Come and see.

She runs across the bridge with EDWARD *and* ALICE.

ALEXANDER (*calling after her*). Who's that singing?

ISOBEL. Melissa!

ISOBEL *and the* CHILDREN *disappear into the cottage.*

THOMAS. You know, when you said you lived in a big house, I thought you meant one this size.

ALEXANDER. You are all right, aren't you, Thomas? I mean, you're not unhappy here?

THOMAS. Unhappy? How could anyone be unhappy in a place like this?

They start across the bridge.

Scene Twelve

ALEXANDER *and* THOMAS *enter the cottage.* ISOBEL *is waiting for them. It is almost like a doll's house, with perfect, small-sized versions of everything.* MELISSA *is sitting at the virginals, playing and singing. The* CHILDREN *are sitting on a rug, playing with their dolls.*

ALEXANDER *watches* MELISSA *playing, with a slight frown on his face. She finishes the piece.* ISOBEL *and* THOMAS *break into applause.*

ISOBEL. That was lovely!

THOMAS. It was!

ISOBEL. Doesn't she play well, Alex?

ALEXANDER. Yes.

MELISSA. It's only because I practise a great deal.

THOMAS *approaches her.*

THOMAS. And tell me, do you see colours when you play different notes?

MELISSA (*puzzled*). No.

ALICE. Look at our dolls, Thomas.

THOMAS. Let's see. They're splendid. But what happened to the cradle?

EDWARD. Her doll was too fat.

THOMAS. I can mend this for you, if you like.

ALICE. Yes, please!

ISOBEL. Could you really, Thomas?

THOMAS. Of course. My Da's a carpenter. I can mend anything.

EDWARD. Can you do it now?

THOMAS. I'll have a go . . .

THOMAS *begins trying to fix the cradle.* ALEXANDER *has crossed to the virginals, where* MELISSA *is sorting out her music. He stares down at the instrument.*

ALEXANDER. It looks so small and shabby. It used to feel like a whole world was opening up before me when I lifted the lid.

MELISSA. Would you play something? I'd very much like to hear you.

ALEXANDER. No. I couldn't. There aren't enough octaves and it's horribly out of tune. Nothing could sound good on this.

MELISSA. Oh. I'm sorry to have inflicted it on you.

MELISSA *moves away, offended.* ISOBEL *comes rushing up to* ALEXANDER *before he can respond.*

ISOBEL. Oh, play something, will you? Play some dancing music so we can practise for the ball. Oh, please. Please. Please, Alex.

ALEXANDER. All right then. Just some dancing music.

ALICE. Hurrah!

ALEXANDER *sits down at the virginals and begins to play some lively music.*

ISOBEL. Dance! Dance! Everyone has to dance!

THOMAS *and the* CHILDREN *join in.* MELISSA *watches for a few moments before* ISOBEL *comes and grabs her and whirls her around and around so that she can't help but smile.* ALEXANDER *begins to sing to the music too. A face appears at the window, unseen by any of them. It is* MESHAK. *He stares in wonder at the fairy-tale house and the dancing* CHILDREN. *Then his eyes settle on* MELISSA *and his expression changes. Her auburn hair, her blue eyes, her beautiful smile – it is his angel. And then there is no one else but her, spinning and spinning in rapture. She is breathing, living.*

MESHAK. Angel. My angel . . .

OTIS*'s voice cuts through the sound of the music.*

OTIS. Meshak!

MESHAK *doesn't go – he has to watch her.*

Meshak! Get here before I break your bones!

MESHAK *finally runs off to find him.*

Scene Thirteen

In the drawing room. Evening. ISOBEL, ALICE *and* EDWARD *are singing a simple song – 'Three Children Sliding'.* MELISSA *is accompanying them.* LADY ASHBROOK *and* THOMAS *are watching with delight.* ALEXANDER *is smiling too.* MRS MILCOTE *is showing a suitable amount of appreciation, whilst glancing at* ALEXANDER *from time to time.* MRS LYNCH *watches as a* SERVANT *places a tray of tea before* LADY ASHBROOK. *The* SERVANT *goes.*

CHILDREN.
>Three children sliding on the ice, upon a summer's day,
>It so fell out, they all fell in, the rest they ran away,
>The rest they ran, the rest they ran away.
>
>Now had these children been at home, or sliding on dry
>   ground,
>Ten thousand pound to one penny, they had not all been
>   drowned,
>They had not all, they had not all been drowned.
>
>You parents all that children have, and you that have got none,
>If you would keep them safe abroad, pray keep them safe
>   at home,
>Pray keep them safe, pray keep them safe at home.

The audience claps.

LADY ASHBROOK. Bravo! Well done, all of you.

MRS MILCOTE. Very good.

ALICE. Edward went wrong.

EDWARD. Alice went wrong.

ISOBEL. You both went wrong. I was the only one doing it properly.

ALICE. Sing your song, Thomas.

THOMAS (*alarmed*). What?

ALICE. Sing the funny song you sang before.

EDWARD. You know. When we were in the bedroom.

ALICE. About the fishing.

THOMAS (*glancing at* ALEXANDER). Oh, that.

ISOBEL. Please, Thomas. I haven't heard it.

THOMAS. Oh. I don't think I'd better. Alexander doesn't like me to sing my songs.

MELISSA (*pointedly*). Really? I'd like to hear it.

ALEXANDER. Of course you should sing it, if you want to.

LADY ASHBROOK. Why don't you both sing one of the songs you've been learning at the cathedral? I'd love to hear something.

ISOBEL. Oh yes, do.

THOMAS. We could do 'Oh death, why must we sing?'

ALEXANDER. All right.

ALEXANDER finds the note on the harpsichord and they begin to sing 'Oh Death, Where Is Thy Sting'. LADY ASHBROOK's face fills with joy. But half-way through the song a man enters and stands in the doorway, listening. ALEXANDER sees him and stops singing. THOMAS stops too (eventually). The man, distinguished and robust, is SIR WILLIAM ASHBROOK.

SIR WILLIAM. Go on, go on.

LADY ASHBROOK. William! Good heavens! I wasn't expecting you until tomorrow.

The CHILDREN *and* MRS MILCOTE *have all stood – as though to attention.*

SIR WILLIAM. Ship got in early. Made good time. Mrs Milcote. Children.

MRS MILCOTE. Sir William.

CHILDREN. Good evening, Papa.

SIR WILLIAM approaches ALEXANDER and makes a slight bow to him.

SIR WILLIAM. Good to have you back with us.

ALEXANDER. Thank you, Sir.

SIR WILLIAM. Still got the voice then.

ALEXANDER. Yes, Sir.

SIR WILLIAM. Not for much longer though, eh?

ALEXANDER looks shocked and angry.

And who's our other little songbird?

LADY ASHBROOK. This is Alexander's friend – Thomas Ledbury.

THOMAS gives a bow.

THOMAS. How do you do, Sir?

SIR WILLIAM. Ledbury – do we know your people?

LADY ASHBROOK. Thomas is at the choir school with Alexander. He has come to stay for the week.

SIR WILLIAM. Has he now? Well, I daresay we've got room for a little one. As long as you promise not to drink all my sherry.

THOMAS. I'm more of a whisky man myself, Sir.

SIR WILLIAM. Very good. Very good. Yes. And what do you want to do when you grow up?

THOMAS. I want to be a musician, Sir.

SIR WILLIAM. Do you indeed? And what does your father say to that?

THOMAS. He wanted me to be a ship's carpenter like him . . .

SIR WILLIAM. Of course.

THOMAS. . . . but now he's happy about me being a musician. He says a man's lucky indeed if he can spend his life doing what he loves.

There is an awkward pause.

SIR WILLIAM. A nice sentiment, I'm sure.

He starts to leave.

I'll have my supper in the study.

LADY ASHBROOK. Yes, dear.

He goes. MRS LYNCH *follows him out.* ALEXANDER *is standing very still.*

MRS MILCOTE. Melissa, why don't you and Alexander play a duet together? I think they would play very well together, don't you, My Lady?

ALEXANDER *suddenly rushes out after his father.*

LADY ASHBROOK. Alex?

Scene Fourteen

SIR WILLIAM *is walking to his study.* ALEXANDER *runs up behind him.*

ALEXANDER. Papa?

SIR WILLIAM. Yes?

ALEXANDER *hesitates.*

Well, spit it out.

ALEXANDER. Have you received a letter from Dr Smith? He said he had written to you.

LADY ASHBROOK *hurries up.*

LADY ASHBROOK. Your father is tired now, Alex. You can discuss this in the morning.

SIR WILLIAM. Yes. I have. Damned impertinent, telling me what to do with my own boy. It's out of the question, of course. As soon as that voice cracks, I want you back at Ashbrook.

ALEXANDER. But I have to go on studying my music. How can I do that if I come back here?

SIR WILLIAM. A bargain is a bargain. I made a bargain with you – against my better judgment, mind – but I stuck to it and you will stick to it too. Music is all very well for your friend in there, but it won't do for you.

ALEXANDER. But . . .

SIR WILLIAM. What?

ALEXANDER *dares not continue.*

Tinkle around to entertain the ladies by all means, but your first duty should be and must be to this estate and to the business of this family. Look at me! I do not wish to hear another word on the matter. Is that understood?

ALEXANDER. Yes, Sir.

SIR WILLIAM *leaves.* ALEXANDER *turns to his mother.*

Go and talk to him.

LADY ASHBROOK. Alex . . .

ALEXANDER. I'm not leaving the cathedral. I don't care what he says.

LADY ASHBROOK. You know how difficult it was for me to persuade him to let you go at all. It was always on the understanding that once your voice broke . . .

ALEXANDER. This isn't about my voice. It's everything. I've started writing music of my own.

LADY ASHBROOK. That's wonderful. It really is. You know how proud of you I am.

ALEXANDER. I have to study every day. I have to have a teacher – a brilliant teacher.

LADY ASHBROOK. No one is saying you won't be able to play from time to time – or write if that's what you want to do. In fact you must write if you . . .

ALEXANDER. It's not enough! Why don't you understand? It's like if someone said you had to lose the thing that meant most to you. How would you feel if someone took Edward and Alice away and said you could never see them again?

LADY ASHBROOK. Now, stop it! Really. Why must you always be so extreme? You have to start accepting what your father has said. For all our sakes.

He walks off. LADY ASHBROOK's *face is full of concern.*

Scene Fifteen

Late evening. MELISSA *is in her mother's bedroom.*

MELISSA. It was humiliating and embarrassing.

MRS MILCOTE. What is so embarrassing about suggesting you play a duet?

MELISSA. Don't pretend, Mother, please. You ought to know now that he has no interest in me whatsoever. And I have none in him.

Outside the room, MRS LYNCH *is passing by. She stops and listens.*

MRS MILCOTE. Then you're a very silly girl. A very, very, silly, silly girl. Alexander Ashbrook is one of the most eligible young men in Gloucestershire.

MELISSA. He is surly and proud.

MRS MILCOTE. Proud? Proud? I should say he has a right to be.

MELISSA. And arrogant.

MRS MILCOTE. Heir to all this and good-looking to boot? And you, Melissa Milcote, have the excellent good fortune to be brought to his attention. A lot of girls would give their eye teeth for that.

MELISSA. Well, I am not a lot of girls.

MRS MILCOTE. Your whole future depends upon your marrying well.

MELISSA. I am fifteen, Mother.

MRS MILCOTE. And almost a woman. I was married at eighteen and Lady Ashbrook, unless I'm much mistaken, was married younger. Your dear father, God rest his soul, left us nothing, absolutely nothing. All we have to offer are your breeding and your good looks.

MELISSA. You make me sound like a horse.

MRS MILCOTE. Now you really are being silly. You must stop being so touchy, Melissa. Humiliation and embarrassment in these matters are the privilege of the rich and powerful – not the likes of us.

Scene Sixteen

ALEXANDER *and* THOMAS *are in* ALEXANDER's *bedroom.*

ALEXANDER. I wish I wasn't Alexander Ashbrook! I wish I'd been born with nothing!

THOMAS. Steady on.

ALEXANDER. I just want to stay in a big room and write music. And not go anywhere or see anyone!

Pause.

THOMAS. You might get a bit fed up.

ALEXANDER. I wouldn't!

This is the first time ALEXANDER *has really shouted at* THOMAS. *But* THOMAS *is not put off.*

THOMAS. You have to talk to him again. You have to make him listen.

ALEXANDER. He doesn't know how to listen.

THOMAS. Did you tell him you've started writing music? I
mean, playing the harpsichord or the fiddle, that's one thing,
but being a composer . . . you could be the next Handel!
Why don't you play him your song?

ALEXANDER. I don't want him to hear it. It wouldn't mean
anything to him.

THOMAS. Play it to your mother then.

ALEXANDER *doesn't respond.*

You can't just give up. You have to do something. Alex?

ALEXANDER. The ball.

THOMAS. What about it?

ALEXANDER. There'll be lots of musicians here.

THOMAS. There's bound to be.

ALEXANDER. I could sing it for her. I could write out all the
different parts and give it to the musicians.

THOMAS. Yes! That's it! And it'll sound wonderful. And
everyone will smack your dad on the back and tell him he's
got a son who's gifted!

ALEXANDER. I don't know.

THOMAS. What?

ALEXANDER. I don't know if I dare.

THOMAS. Of course you do. Of course you dare. It's a
brilliant idea, Alex. It could change everything.

Pause.

ALEXANDER. We'd better start now then.

THOMAS. Yes.

ALEXANDER. Let's start on second violin. Play me the top
line, will you?

Scene Seventeen

Below stairs, MRS LYNCH *goes to the back door and opens it
quietly.* OTIS *is there. He grins.*

OTIS. Need any knives sharpening, Ma'am?

She moves aside and lets him in, then locks the door.

MRS LYNCH. Go to the kitchen.

OTIS. Not this time. Take me above stairs.

MRS LYNCH. You know I can't do that.

OTIS. Come on. I'll be very quiet. I'll do as I'm told.

MRS LYNCH. They've only just gone to bed.

OTIS. Not scared are you, Mrs Lynch?

Scene Eighteen

MRS LYNCH *and* OTIS *enter the drawing room.* MRS LYNCH *is carrying a candelabra which she sets down.* OTIS *looks about him, smiling.*

OTIS. This is more like it.

MRS LYNCH. If we're found in here I'll lose my job.

OTIS. Maybe that wouldn't be so bad.

MRS LYNCH. It's taken me years to earn the trust I have.

OTIS *walks about, taking in all the paintings and ornaments.*

OTIS. Nice.

MRS LYNCH. You got my message about the ball?

OTIS. Saturday.

MRS LYNCH. The players are staying on in the village for a week. There'll be plenty of trade for you.

OTIS. Now let me guess . . .

He crosses the room and sits in a fine chair.

His Lordship's chair.

MRS LYNCH. Don't get it dirty.

OTIS. What do you reckon? Lord Gardiner of Gloucester? What do you reckon?

MRS LYNCH. I reckon you had better keep dreaming.

OTIS. Well, I reckon that's where you're wrong. What if I told you that in a year or two, you and I could be sitting pretty in a place like this of our own?

MRS LYNCH. What are you talking about?

OTIS. Come here.

MRS LYNCH. Why?

OTIS. For God's sake. Just come here, woman.

She goes to him.

Pick my pocket.

MRS LYNCH. You're so cheap.

OTIS. I mean it.

She does so, and draws out a purse heavy with coins.

MRS LYNCH. What's this?

OTIS. This, Mrs Lynch, is what I've taken from just two of your young ladies – Miss Price, was it? And the other one in Stroud you told me to visit.

MRS LYNCH. So much?

OTIS. So much. It's more money than I've ever seen. And half of it's yours. You're a clever one and no mistake. This Coram idea's a gold mine. This is before we've even started going back to them with our little tit-bits of information. Very soon I'll have a list as long as my arm of young ladies who are making regular contributions to our future life.

MRS LYNCH. Lives. Our future lives.

OTIS. There'll be no more trawling around the workhouses, no more pots and pans, no more serving. Now, tell me you're not excited.

MRS LYNCH. Don't get overconfident.

OTIS. What can go wrong? You said yourself, none of 'em'll go looking for the brats. These aren't the usual snivelling parlour maids, these value their reputations too much.

MRS LYNCH. Even so. Tread carefully, Otis.

OTIS. Whatever you say.

They kiss passionately.

MRS LYNCH. Miss Price's baby . . .

OTIS. What about it?

MRS LYNCH. Did it live for long?

OTIS. As long as all the rest.

He kisses her again. She suddenly stands and moves towards the door.

MRS LYNCH. I'll lock the door.

OTIS. Leave it.

They stare at each other for a few moments, then she goes back to him and they fall into each other's arms.

Scene Nineteen

Outside, on the lawn, in the darkness, MESHAK is gazing up at MELISSA's window. He can see her moving about – it looks as though she is practising her dancing in anticipation of the ball.

MESHAK. I'm here. Can you see me, Angel?

In his bedroom, his head full of music, ALEXANDER stares out of the window. He sees MESHAK and wonders what he is doing – what he is looking at. Subconsciously, a picture of MELISSA flashes through his brain – a sudden desire for her, or a sense that their fates are intertwined. It disturbs him.

THOMAS. Come on, Alex!

ALEXANDER turns away from the window.

Scene Twenty

The ballroom – splendid and shining, a feast of light and mirrors and flowers. MUSICIANS are settling themselves into the gallery. MRS LYNCH is directing STAFF in last-minute touches. ISOBEL enters, dressed in her ball gown, beside herself with excitement. MELISSA arrives – looking beautiful.

ISOBEL. There you are! How do I look?

MELISSA. Enchanting.

ISOBEL. Do I really? Do you really think?

MELISSA. You look like a princess.

ISOBEL. And you look lovely too. I'm so excited I can hardly breathe.

MELISSA. This bodice is so tight I can hardly breathe.

ISOBEL. You won't leave me alone, will you?

MELISSA. Of course not. I'll stay with you all the time.

ISOBEL. Unless someone asks me to dance. Then you could just go away a bit. There's Thomas!

THOMAS enters. He is dressed in a neat little velvet suit with knickerbockers and a frilly shirt.

Thomas! You look adorable!

THOMAS. I feel a bit silly.

MELISSA. It's very sweet.

THOMAS. I'm just glad my Da's not here. Where's Alex?

MELISSA. He hasn't graced us with his presence yet.

ISOBEL. Guests! Let's go and watch.

They rush off. In the gallery the MUSICIANS *strike up.* SIR WILLIAM *and* LADY ASHBROOK *appear in the doorway and begin to welcome the* GUESTS. *Across the room,* MRS MILCOTE *enters and smiles with delight at her surroundings. She sees* MRS LYNCH *pass by.*

MRS MILCOTE. I must say, you have surpassed yourself, Mrs Lynch.

MRS LYNCH. Thank you, Madam.

MRS MILCOTE. My late husband and I used to entertain a great deal, so I understand the effort involved. Luckily we were blessed with an excellent housekeeper. (*Looking across to the door.*) Who is that with Mr and Mrs Claymore?

MRS LYNCH looks. MR CLAYMORE has just entered and is speaking to LORD ASHBROOK. Beside him are two ladies – one, his WIFE, the other is MISS PRICE.

MRS LYNCH. Mr Claymore's ward. Miss Price.

MRS MILCOTE. A pretty girl, but so thin. Is she sickening?

MRS LYNCH. I'm afraid I don't know.

MRS LYNCH *moves away to continue her work.*

ALEXANDER *enters, carrying some music. He glances about to make sure his father isn't watching and then makes his way up to the gallery and begins to talk to one of the* MUSICIANS.

MESHAK*'s face appears at a window. He looks about for* MELISSA *but he cannot see her and he disappears again.*

PEOPLE *are dancing now as more and more* guests *arrive.* ISOBEL, MELISSA *and* THOMAS *enter.*

MR CLAYMORE *makes a great show of being in awe of* MELISSA*'s beauty and asks her to dance. She curtsies politely but refuses and walks away.*

MISS PRICE *sees* MRS LYNCH *and catches her eye.* MRS LYNCH *passes close to her.*

MISS PRICE. Have you seen him?

MRS LYNCH. Go to the terrace.

MRS LYNCH *walks out through the French windows onto the moonlit terrace. After a moment,* MISS PRICE *appears.*

MISS PRICE. Have you seen the Coram Man? I have to know if she's all right.

MRS LYNCH. I know he's in the district. I will ask him to come to you.

MISS PRICE. Thank you. I have to know.

MRS LYNCH *starts to go back inside.*

Mrs Lynch? Is there anything you can give me . . . to stop me . . . I'm so scared that another baby will come.

MRS LYNCH. You have to stop him touching you.

MISS PRICE. How? He does what he likes. I'm dependent on him.

MRS LYNCH. If you think there's the slightest chance you are with child, you must come to me immediately. There are things I can give you. Things I can try to stop the baby. You understand?

MISS PRICE *nods.* MRS LYNCH *goes inside. After a few moments* MISS PRICE *goes in too.*

In the ballroom, SIR WILLIAM *is standing with* MRS MILCOTE. *He notices* ALEXANDER *talking to the* MUSICIANS.

SIR WILLIAM. Alexander! What are you doing there?

ALEXANDER. I'm sorry, Sir, I was just . . .

SIR WILLIAM. Let's have you out on that dance floor.

ALEXANDER. I don't like dancing.

MRS MILCOTE. Melissa is without a partner, look.

SIR WILLIAM. Capital. She'll do. Go and ask her.

ALEXANDER. I'd rather not.

SIR WILLIAM. Nonsense. Half the men in this room would rather not but we just have to get on with it. Go on, boy.

ALEXANDER *strides over to* MELISSA, *his jaw set with irritation. She is standing alone.*

ALEXANDER. Will you dance with me?

MELISSA. With you?

She glances round and sees her mother's expectant face.

I'll dance with you if you say please.

ALEXANDER *looks very surprised. He thinks for a moment, then says:*

ALEXANDER. Please.

MELISSA. Very well. Thank you.

She takes his hand and he leads her onto the floor. Her heart is pounding. This is the first time she has danced in public before. As they take up a position and wait for the beat, she smiles at him nervously. And then they begin to dance. ALEXANDER *is rigid and expressionless.*

ISOBEL *is now dancing with* MR CLAYMORE. *She is giggling and adoring the attention.* LADY ASHBROOK *is watching and smiling to see* ISOBEL *so happy.*

MELISSA *begins to realise that* ALEXANDER*'s heart is not in the dance. It reaches the point where he is being positively rude and making her look foolish.*

If you don't like to dance, why did you ask me?

ALEXANDER. For the same reason I do everything around here; because my father told me to.

MELISSA *stops dancing abruptly and stares up at him, right into his eyes.*

What?

She continues to stare. She is fighting back tears.

What?

MELISSA *starts to run off. He catches her arm.*

Melissa?

She shakes his arm off and runs outside onto the terrace. He follows her out, looking confused.

MESHAK, *who has been watching them dancing from the terrace, ducks into the shadows.*

What's wrong?

MELISSA. If you think I want any part in this, you're wrong!

ALEXANDER. What do you mean?

MELISSA. Do you think I don't hate this too? Being pushed together, being forced in front of your eyes like some prize pony!

ALEXANDER. I . . .

MELISSA. You are not the only person in this house who feels things, you're not the only sensitive person, you're just the only one who's so wrapped up in your own feelings that you don't notice anyone else's!

Silence.

ALEXANDER. I'm sorry. I hadn't . . . I'm very sorry. I don't want to upset you.

Pause.

MELISSA. I just wish . . .

ALEXANDER. What?

MELISSA. I just wish they'd leave me alone. Trapped. It's feeling trapped into things. I hate it.

ALEXANDER. Yes. I really am sorry.

MELISSA. So am I.

They are quiet for a moment. The music drifts out from the house.

ALEXANDER. If I asked you again, would you dance with me? Out here? We could dance just for us.

MELISSA *nods.* ALEXANDER *approaches her.*

Please. Would you please dance with me, please?

MELISSA *laughs. She takes his hand and they begin to dance. This time it feels different. There is something between them – they both feel very aware of their bodies, of their hands touching and they look into each other's eyes.*

MESHAK *cannot stand to see this. He suddenly collapses to the ground in a 'dead' state.* ALEXANDER *and* MELISSA *hear him fall and look to see what has happened.*

MELISSA. Oh. Do you think he's all right?

ALEXANDER. I'm not sure.

MELISSA *kneels beside him and touches his forehead.*

MELISSA. Poor thing.

ALEXANDER. I've seen him before. I think I should get help.

Suddenly OTIS *appears.*

OTIS. Just leave him. He'll get up in a minute.

ALEXANDER *and* MELISSA *stand up and look at* OTIS. *But at this moment,* THOMAS *appears.*

THOMAS. There you are. The musician's master was looking for you. He says it's time. Come on.

MELISSA. Time for what?

ALEXANDER. Come with me.

He takes her hand and they go back inside. OTIS *kicks* MESHAK.

OTIS. Get up, cretin!

MRS LYNCH *comes outside.*

MRS LYNCH. You shouldn't do that.

She crosses to MESHAK *and watches him.*

I saw something like it once. A young gentleman in France. He didn't live long.

OTIS. He'll live to a ripe old age, just you watch. I should have drowned him at birth.

MRS LYNCH. But you didn't.

OTIS. Maybe it's true what they say – blood's thicker than water.

MESHAK comes out of his 'dead' state and gets to his feet, shakily.

MESHAK. Angel loves Meshak.

OTIS. You and your angels. There ain't no angels!

MESHAK runs off, distressed. At the same time, MISS PRICE comes onto the terrace.

MISS PRICE. You found him . . .

But MR CLAYMORE appears in the doorway behind her. MISS PRICE looks at him in alarm.

CLAYMORE. What are you doing out here? Come back inside.

MISS PRICE goes back in. MR CLAYMORE looks at OTIS and at MRS LYNCH.

MRS LYNCH. Good evening, Sir.

They stare at each other for a few moments, then he goes back inside.

In the ballroom the MUSICIANS come to the end of a song. ALEXANDER stands up in the gallery and addresses the guests.

ALEXANDER. Ladies and gentlemen.

The GUESTS look up in surprise. THOMAS beams up at him. MELISSA watches anxiously. SIR WILLIAM is standing with LADY ASHBROOK. He frowns.

SIR WILLIAM. What on earth . . . ?

ALEXANDER. As you all know, it is my mother's birthday tomorrow.

A ripple of applause goes round the room.

As a surprise for her, I would like to sing for her. I would like to sing a song which I have written and arranged myself.

The GUESTS *make impressed and appreciative noises.* SIR WILLIAM *is rigid with anger. He is about to step forward and speak.* LADY ASHBROOK *puts a hand on his arm.*

LADY ASHBROOK (*quietly*). Don't. Please.

The MUSICIANS *begin to play and* ALEXANDER *begins to sing – 'I Will Praise Thee'. His voice and the music are so beautiful that tears come to eyes and mouths fall open.* MELISSA *steps forward – closer and closer to him.*

ALEXANDER.
I will praise thee, praise thee, O Lord,
With my whole heart,
I'll praise, praise, praise thee, O Lord,
I will praise thee, I will praise thee,
I will praise thee with my whole heart.
I shall show forth all thy marvellous works,
I will be glad and rejoice in thee,
And rejoice, rejoice,
I'll be glad and rejoice in thee . . .

He nears the end of the song. But suddenly his voice gives way. He tries to keep singing but it happens again. He tries again, but the sound he makes is low and rough.

The MUSICIANS *are not sure what to do. Gradually they stop playing. He tries one more time. It is no use. He stares down at his feet, breathing hard. There is silence for a moment.*

LADY ASHBROOK (*going to him*). That was beautiful.

SIR WILLIAM. Excellent, Alexander. I never heard you sing so well. Ladies and gentleman, it seems we have another cause to celebrate.

A round of applause goes up. ALEXANDER *looks at his father, who smiles triumphantly.*

Scene Twenty-One

SIR WILLIAM *and* LADY ASHBROOK *are in the drawing room when* ALEXANDER *rushes up to them.*

ALEXANDER. What's happening?

LADY ASHBROOK. Let's go and sit down, Alexander . . .

ALEXANDER. Was that Thomas? Was Thomas in that carriage?

SIR WILLIAM. Gone back to Gloucester. Your timing was excellent. Saved yourself the journey.

LADY ASHBROOK. Alex . . .

ALEXANDER. You can't do this! Why didn't you let me say goodbye?

LADY ASHBROOK. Because we knew you would get upset.

ALEXANDER. You can't do this! I want to go back.

ISOBEL *and* MELISSA *appear and watch with alarm.*

SIR WILLIAM. Well, you can't.

ALEXANDER. I have to! I have music I want to . . .

SIR WILLIAM. No! My God, I wish I'd never let you near the place! Now you and I have four years of catching up to do, so get into your riding gear. You'll ride with me to inspect the mill.

ALEXANDER. No.

SIR WILLIAM. I beg your pardon?

LADY ASHBROOK. Alex . . .

ALEXANDER. I have work to do on my music.

SIR WILLIAM slaps his face. ALEXANDER *stares at him, struggling to control himself. Then he goes to step past him but* SIR WILLIAM *stands in his way.*

Get out of my way.

SIR WILLIAM. How dare you?

ALEXANDER. Well I do! I do dare!

He pushes past SIR WILLIAM *who immediately charges after him.*

LADY ASHBROOK. William, no!

ALEXANDER *storms into the drawing room and sits down at the harpsichord. He begins to play but* SIR WILLIAM *appears beside him and brings the lid crashing down.* ALEXANDER *just manages to pull his fingers free in time. He stares at his father in anger and disbelief.*

SIR WILLIAM. Get it out of here! Mrs Lynch! Mrs Lynch! I want this out! And all the rest, out!

MRS LYNCH *comes hurrying up.*

I want every musical instrument out of this house!

LADY ASHBROOK. William, please . . .

SIR WILLIAM. Every last one!

ALEXANDER. No!

SIR WILLIAM. Every pipe, every fiddle, every drum, every blasted one!

MRS LYNCH. Yes, Sir.

ALEXANDER *gets up suddenly and strides out of the room.*

ISOBEL. Alex? Alex?

But he walks past her as if she isn't there. MELISSA *is aghast.*

Scene Twenty-Two

We are plunged into ALEXANDER*'s head – full of music and colours and memories of raised voices crashing in, then fading away. He hears himself singing in his clear treble voice. He is desperate and angry. It rises to fever pitch before he collapses face down on his bed, exhausted and wretched.*

Night. MELISSA *comes silently to the door of* ALEXANDER*'s bedroom.*

MELISSA (*whispering*). Alexander?

He doesn't reply.

Alexander, it's Melissa.

He looks round at her.

Can I talk to you?

Pause.

ALEXANDER. Yes.

She crosses to his bed and sits down.

MELISSA. It's the cruellest thing I've ever known.

ALEXANDER. I'm going out of my mind. I swear it. I swear I will go mad. I don't know what I am without music. I don't know why to move. Why to breathe.

Pause.

MELISSA. Come with me.

ALEXANDER. What?

MELISSA. I want you to come with me. Trust me.

ALEXANDER. Where are we going?

MELISSA. To Waterside. Be very quiet. Mrs Lynch hears everything.

Scene Twenty-Three

Waterside. MELISSA *and* ALEXANDER *enter.* MELISSA's *candle throws shadowy light around the room. She walks to a corner and pulls away a sheet to reveal the old virginals.* ALEXANDER *gasps. He hurries towards it.*

MELISSA. I hid it.

ALEXANDER *is overwhelmed.*

I know it isn't much, and it's out of tune . . .

ALEXANDER. It's enough. It's enough.

MELISSA. If we keep it in this corner, I don't think the children will take any notice of it. And as long as you only come here at night . . .

ALEXANDER. I don't know how to thank you.

MELISSA. Just play something.

ALEXANDER *plays.* MELISSA *watches, thrilled that he is happy.*

ALEXANDER. I can stand anything . . . I can stand mills and ships and harvests as long as I can do this.

MELISSA. And I'll make sure you have paper and ink and anything you need. And you can give me things for safe-keeping.

ALEXANDER. I'll come here every single night.

MELISSA. Yes.

He stares at her.

ALEXANDER. You've saved me.

MELISSA. I couldn't bear to see you unhappy.

ALEXANDER. You're wonderful.

He kisses her, tentatively at first but she kisses him back and soon they are kissing passionately.

At the window, MESHAK's face appears, white and shocked.

ALEXANDER *draws* MELISSA *out of Waterside and into the woods. In the darkness, he takes her in his arms and covers her in kisses. They sink to the floor and make love – following their instincts, not thinking about what they are doing.*

MESHAK *has followed them and watches until he can bear it no longer. His rage and hurt cannot be contained. For a moment we fear for* MELISSA *and* ALEXANDER, *but then he rushes back to Waterside. He charges up to the virginals and smashes it to pieces.*

MESHAK. *My* angel!

Scene Twenty-Four

The same night. OTIS *is camped in the woods near the cottage, beside a dark, stagnant lake.* MRS LYNCH *arrives and looks about for him.* OTIS *creeps up behind her and covers her eyes.*

OTIS. Who's this sneaking into my lair?

MRS LYNCH. Let go of me, Otis.

He does so, and kisses her, clumsily.

OTIS. Ready to go, my lady?

MRS LYNCH. You've been drinking.

OTIS. Yes I have. Drinking and thinking and laying down plans for you and me.

MRS LYNCH. I've only come to say goodbye.

OTIS. But you're coming with me.

MRS LYNCH. I'm not.

OTIS. Yes you are. You're coming with me to make our fortunes from Mr Coram. The wonderful Mr Coram. There are two more ladies asking for the Coram Man. One of 'em's in Bristol. Bristol! News travels fast, eh? Come with me. We'll put our money in a ship – invest. There's tidy profits to be made . . .

MRS LYNCH. Forget it.

OTIS. We'd be unstoppable – you and me.

MRS LYNCH. I don't throw in my lot with anyone. I learnt that a long time ago.

Pause.

OTIS. Fine. Fine. I'll go on my own. I'm not going to spend the rest of my life grovelling around for scraps even if you are.

MRS LYNCH. I'll get word to you if there's anything for you here.

OTIS. Maybe I won't want to know. Maybe I'll never come back.

MRS LYNCH. That's up to you.

She starts to walk away. He grabs her and kisses her. She kisses him back.

OTIS. Stay the night. Come on. Stay the night.

MRS LYNCH. I couldn't sleep in these woods.

OTIS. You wouldn't have to sleep.

MRS LYNCH. I have to be up before dawn.

OTIS. The highly efficient Mrs Lynch. The oh-so-trustworthy Mrs Lynch. You know all the tricks, don't you? Keep a man keen. Where did you learn all your tricks, eh?

MRS LYNCH. I don't use tricks with you, Otis. If I did, you wouldn't stand a chance.

He suddenly laughs.

I'll see you next time. Yes?

OTIS. Yes.

MRS LYNCH. And remember what I said – be careful.

She leaves. He watches her go, smiling.

Scene Twenty-Five

Two days later. Morning. The whole of Ashbrook House is filled with LADY ASHBROOK*'s cry.*

LADY ASHBROOK. Alex! Alex! No!

SIR WILLIAM bursts from the drawing room into the hallway with a letter in his hand. MRS MILCOTE *and* ISOBEL *come hurrying to him.* MELISSA *follows.* MRS LYNCH *also appears.*

No!

MRS MILCOTE. What is it, Sir William? What has happened?

SIR WILLIAM. It's Alexander. He's gone.

On hearing this, MELISSA *rushes away. She runs to Waterside.*

ISOBEL. Gone?

SIR WILLIAM. Go to her, will you?

MRS MILCOTE and ISOBEL rush into the drawing room.

(*To* MRS LYNCH.) Tell the grooms to saddle the horses.

SIR WILLIAM hurries off.

Scene Twenty-Six

At Waterside, MELISSA *walks in and sees the broken virginals. She is horrified. Next to it she sees a note. She rushes to it and picks it up. It has her name on it. She opens it with trembling hands and reads it.*

MELISSA. God keep you, Alexander.

Scene Twenty-Seven

Several weeks later. MELISSA, ISOBEL, EDWARD *and*
ALICE *are at Waterside. All the old excitement and joy about
the place has gone.* ISOBEL *is playing a game with* EDWARD
and ALICE *using the dolls, but their hearts aren't in it.*
MELISSA *is detached.*

ISOBEL. Well, come on. It seems like I'm the only one
playing. Alice, you have to make her go to the palace.

ALICE. She said she didn't want to go to the palace.

ISOBEL. Well, she does now. What's your man called,
Edward?

EDWARD. He hasn't got a name.

ISOBEL. Of course he has a name.

EDWARD. Alexander. He's called Alexander.

The mention of the name draws everyone up short.

ISOBEL. Think of another name.

EDWARD. No. He's Alexander.

ALICE *starts to cry.*

ISOBEL. Now look what you've done.

MELISSA *goes to* ALICE.

MELISSA. Don't get upset. Wherever he is, I'm sure Alex is
thinking of you.

ISOBEL. No he's not. He's not thinking of us at all. If he was
thinking of us he wouldn't have stayed away for weeks and
weeks without telling us where he is.

MELISSA. I expect he feels he has no choice.

EDWARD. Papa will flog him when he finds him.

ISOBEL. It's mean and selfish and he's ruined everything!

MELISSA. I don't think he's the mean and selfish one. Have
you ever, ever stopped to think what he might be suffering?
Whether he's safe? How he's living? How lonely he must
be?

ISOBEL. It's not my fault!

MELISSA *starts to go.*

Where are you going? I miss him!

MELISSA. I know.

ISOBEL. Why couldn't he have told me he was leaving? I wouldn't have told anyone. I just want him to come back. Where are you going?

MELISSA. I'm sorry. I have to . . . I have to be alone for a while.

ISOBEL. That's all you ever say now! Why do you have to be so miserable? He's not your brother.

MELISSA *leaves. She gets as far away from Waterside as she can before she has to stop to vomit against a tree. She is feeling terrible – physically and emotionally.*

Scene Twenty-Eight

In the drawing room at Ashbrook House. The family are gathered around SIR WILLIAM. *In front of* SIR WILLIAM *there is a desk, on which there is a large bible, a pen and some ink. The mood is sombre.*

SIR WILLIAM. As you are all aware, it is now six months since Alexander saw fit to leave us. And as you are also aware, despite my best efforts, I have been unable to find him.

ISOBEL *sobs.* LADY ASHBROOK *looks down, trying to control herself.*

I can no longer spend my time, nor tie up the valuable resources of this estate in looking for him. It is quite clear that he does not intend to be found. I have therefore reached a decision. This is our family bible. In it are written the names of the Ashbrooks going back for generations.

He picks up the pen, and crosses out ALEXANDER's *name.*

From this day onwards, Alexander does not exist. Edward, you will become the next Lord Ashbrook and I have no doubt that you will be worthy of the title. I never wish to hear mention of Alexander again.

ISOBEL. Mama? (LADY ASHBROOK *will not look at her*).
You can't do this!

SIR WILLIAM. It is done.

ISOBEL *leaves the room in tears.* MRS MILCOTE,
MELISSA *and the children follow her out.* LADY
ASHBROOK *is sitting very still.*

LADY ASHBROOK. I have never wavered in my devotion to
you. And I have wholeheartedly supported you in
everything you do. But it is duty alone now which stops me
from speaking out against this. It is wrong. I bore him. He
is a part of me. And of you. Nothing can ever change that.

She leaves. SIR WILLIAM *stares down at the bible.*

Scene Twenty-Nine

In her bed at Ashbrook House, MELISSA *is tossing and
turning, disturbed by dreams. She dreams she sees*
ALEXANDER *coming towards her, holding a lantern.*

*His face is bright and smiling. But down around his feet there
are babies. A baby crawls up onto* MELISSA's *bed. She
screams with shock and wakens. She is trembling. She just sits
for a moment, trying to steady her heart. She takes stock of her
dream. There is an agonising thought growing in her mind. She
gets out of bed and crosses to a mirror. She looks down at her
stomach, and runs her hands over it. It is growing. She keeps
her hand on it and stares at her reflection.*

Outside the door of her room, MRS LYNCH *appears and
looks in at* MELISSA. MELISSA *sees her.*

MRS LYNCH. Do you want my help?

MELISSA *stares at her.*

You will need it. Tell me when you need it.

MRS LYNCH *goes.* MELISSA *is breathing hard. She turns
to the bed and grabs a blanket and wraps it around herself
to cover the bump. She looks in the mirror to see if it can be
concealed. She sinks to her knees and weeps.*

Scene Thirty

Several months later. In the house, ISOBEL *rushes up to* MRS LYNCH. *She is white-faced and shaking.*

ISOBEL. Mrs Lynch?

MRS LYNCH. Is it Melissa?

ISOBEL (*nodding*). She's at Waterside. She wants you. She's screaming with pain. I think she's dying.

MRS LYNCH. She's not dying. Her baby is coming.

ISOBEL. Baby? What are you talking about?

MRS LYNCH. Melissa is having your brother's baby.

ISOBEL. You're lying.

MRS LYNCH. She is having Alexander's baby. It's the truth.

ISOBEL, *through sheer shock, hits* MRS LYNCH *across the face.* MRS LYNCH *does not flinch.* ISOBEL *clasps her hand over her mouth – horrified at what she has done and what is happening.*

You must be very calm now. You must go back and help her while I fetch her mother and bring the things we need.

ISOBEL. No. She said not her mother. She said not to tell her mother.

MRS LYNCH. She must be told. If anything were to go wrong . . . it's only right that she should be there.

ISOBEL. What will go wrong?

MRS LYNCH. Calm yourself. Go back to her. And tell no one of this. No one.

Scene Thirty-One

At Waterside, MELISSA *is on the ground, struggling with the pain of a contraction.* MESHAK *appears in the open doorway and stares at her, horrified to see her like this. She sees him and her eyes meet his.*

MELISSA. The baby . . .

He darts away, as ISOBEL *comes rushing in and goes straight to* MELISSA. ISOBEL *is struggling to take in the situation.*

ISOBEL. Why didn't you tell me?

MELISSA. Is she coming?

ISOBEL. Yes. Why didn't you tell me?

MELISSA. I didn't want it to be true.

ISOBEL. Alexander's baby.

MELISSA. Oh, hold my hand.

She screams in agony. Outside the window, MESHAK *closes his ears.*

MRS LYNCH, *half-supporting* MRS MILCOTE, *arrives in front of the cottage.*

MRS MILCOTE. Here?

MRS LYNCH. Yes.

MRS MILCOTE. Lord help me, this can't be happening.

MRS LYNCH. Remember, she must not be allowed to hold the baby. She must not become attached to it.

MRS MILCOTE. She can't keep it. Oh, my Lord, what will become of us?

MRS LYNCH. No, she can't keep it. Are we agreed that we will give it to the Coram Man? Look at me. We will give it to the Coram Man?

MRS MILCOTE. Yes. The Coram Man. But . . . but how will he know to come?

MRS LYNCH. He is already here.

They go into the cottage. MELISSA*'s baby is coming.* MRS MILCOTE *rushes to her side.*

MELISSA. I'm sorry. I'm sorry.

MRS MILCOTE *kisses her face and hands.* MRS LYNCH *delivers the baby.* ISOBEL *is crying with shock and joy.* MRS LYNCH *hands the baby to* ISOBEL *while she cuts the umbilical cord. The baby is still and silent.* ISOBEL *is overwhelmed with wonder and love.*

ISOBEL. Look. Oh, look, Melissa. Look.

MELISSA holds out her arms to take her son. But MRS
LYNCH *takes him quickly from* ISOBEL. MRS MILCOTE
takes off her pink shawl and hands it to MRS LYNCH.

MRS MILCOTE. Here . . .

*MRS LYNCH wraps the shawl around the baby and walks
out of the cottage.* MRS MILCOTE *rushes after her.*

Wait!

MRS LYNCH pauses. MRS MILCOTE *takes the baby from
her and cradles it in her arms.*

My grandson. God bless you. God bless you.

She kisses his head. MRS LYNCH *takes him back.*

MRS LYNCH. Tell her it was dead.

MRS MILCOTE looks aghast.

It's the only way. Tell her.

MRS LYNCH rushes off along the path to the lake.
MESHAK *comes out from his hiding place to follow her. He
comes face to face with* MRS MILCOTE *and they both
freeze like frightened animals. Then* MESHAK *runs off
after* MRS LYNCH.

He arrives at the lake in time to see her handing the baby to
OTIS.

Come to me soon. I'll have the money for you.

OTIS. Tonight?

She nods and then rushes back to the cottage. MESHAK
approaches OTIS *cautiously, staring at the baby – his
angel's baby.* OTIS *sees him.*

Here. Bury it with the rest. It's dead anyway.

*MESHAK takes the baby slowly, hardly believing he can
hold it in his hands.* OTIS *thrusts a spade at him.*

Get on with it, you worthless idiot!

*MESHAK stares at his father. All he can see in his eyes are
hatred and contempt. He takes the baby to the lake. He
stares at the baby's face.*

MESHAK. Angel child. Angel child. Wake up. Wake up.

He throws aside the pink shawl, now stained with blood. Gently, he lowers the baby into the water. He takes water in his fingers and sprinkles it on the baby's head.

Wake up.

Suddenly the baby lets out a cry.

Shh, shh. Shh, shh. Mustn't let Da hear.

He puts his finger to the baby's mouth and it stops crying. MESHAK looks round towards OTIS – he is not watching him.

Angel child. Come with Meshak. Safe with Meshak.

He tucks the baby under his jacket and stumbles off into the woods.

Scene Thirty-Two

The following scenes take place under music, so that the words are not heard and only the action tells the story.

In the woods, beside the stagnant lake, the pink shawl blows in the wind. Day turns to night, and night to day. ALICE and EDWARD come running through the woods in winter sunshine. They have found some small skulls and stuck them on the end of sticks. They are chasing each other with them.

MRS MILCOTE comes along after them and sees what they are playing with. Horrified, she takes the skulls off them. ALICE points to where they found them – near to the water. MRS MILCOTE sends the children back to the house. Slowly, she approaches the spot which ALICE pointed to and crouches down. There are more bones. She stands and backs away. Then she sees the shawl. It is lying in mud nearby. She picks it up and sees the blood on it. She doubles over with shock and grief. Then she hurriedly bundles it up and tucks it inside her coat. She rushes back to the house.

Scene Thirty-Three

MEN *with dogs are digging up the ground by the lake.* MR
CLAYMORE *is directing them.* SIR WILLIAM *and* LADY
ASHBROOK *arrive. Two* MEN *pass by them, carefully
carrying cloths containing human remains.*

CLAYMORE (*to the* MEN). Take them to the church and lay
them out beside the others. (*Addressing the* ASHBROOKS.)
My Lord. Lady Ashbrook.

SIR WILLIAM. You've found more then?

CLAYMORE. That's nine so far.

LADY ASHBROOK. It's too horrible. On our own land.

SIR WILLIAM. But you have someone?

CLAYMORE. We've apprehended a fellow called Otis
Gardiner. A tinker. He's known to camp in these woods.
Two local women have come forward to say they paid him
to take their babies from them.

LADY ASHBROOK. Paid him?

CLAYMORE. He was supposed to take them somewhere safe.

SIR WILLIAM. For God's sake.

LADY ASHBROOK. Those poor women.

SIR WILLIAM. Has he confessed? This tinker?

CLAYMORE. Not yet. But if the evidence against him
continues to mount, I'll hang him anyway – confession or
no confession.

Scene Thirty-Four

In the local court room, OTIS *is in the dock.* MR CLAYMORE
is presiding. The room and the gallery are packed with
PEOPLE. *Amongst them are* SIR WILLIAM *and* LADY
ASHBROOK.

MRS LYNCH *is also there, sitting quietly to one side, watching.
The room is in uproar – people are shouting and shaking their
fists and throwing things at* OTIS. OTIS *is sneering.*

CLAYMORE. Silence! Silence!

The room quietens.

Otis Gardiner, you have been found guilty on three counts of murder. Only our Lord God can know how many other heinous acts you have committed in the name of greed and cruelty.

There is another outbreak of shouting. The following lines rise above the music:

Silence! Otis Gardiner, it is my duty to sentence you to death by hanging! Take him to the gaol.

OTIS. What about them as gave me the brats? Why aren't they guilty? Out of sight, out of mind, eh? Pay me to do their dirty work!

OTIS *is dragged away with the* CROWD *jeering and screaming at him as he goes.* MR CLAYMORE *stands and goes out of a door at the back of the room.* MRS LYNCH *stands up and follows him out. She is clearly going to speak to him.*

Scene Thirty-Five

OTIS, *blind-folded and gagged, is led to the gibbet. A* HANGMAN *places a noose around his neck. And he is hanged.*

End of Act One.

ACT TWO

Scene One

1750. The Coram Foundling Hospital. The CORAM CHILDREN *are singing the Coram Hymn.*

CHILDREN.
> Left on the world's bleak waste forlorn,
> In sin conceived, to sorrow born,
> By guilt and shame fordoomed to share
> No mother's love, no father's care,
> No guide the devious maze to tread,
> Above no friendly shelter spread.

Two boys – one black, TOBY, *and one white,* AARON – *break away from the other* CHILDREN *and peer into a very large, imposing room. At one end of the room there is a group of anxious and desperate-looking* MOTHERS *holding babies. At the other end of the room there is a group of wealthy* LADIES *and* GENTLEMEN *who are watching the proceedings with interest. In the middle of the room there is a desk, behind which a* GOVERNOR *sits, with a* LADY *to each side of him. On the desk there is a basket covered with a cloth. The two* LADIES *have pens and paper before them.*

GOVERNOR (*addressing the* MOTHERS). Those of you who draw a white ball from the basket, have been successful. Your infants will undergo a medical examination and, if deemed fit, will enter the Coram Hospital.

Those of you who draw a red ball must await the outcome of those said examinations to see if a place becomes available once more.

Those of you who draw a black ball, have been unsuccessful and you must take your infants away. Today we are offering three places. May God be with you all.

LADY (*nodding to a* MOTHER). Step forward, please.

The MOTHER *approaches the desk. She puts her hand under the cloth into the basket and draws out a ball. It is red. One of the* LADIES *records this.*

GOVERNOR. Step to the side please, Miss.

She does so. The LADY *nods to the next* MOTHER *who comes forward. She draws a ball from the basket. It is black. A sympathetic noise comes from the wealthy* LADIES.

MOTHER. No. Let me try again. Please. I'll come back tomorrow.

LADY. The pressure of numbers does not permit that.

MOTHER. He's a lovely boy. He's healthy and beautiful.

LADY. Step aside please, Miss.

MOTHER. This isn't fair!

GOVENOR. It is the fairest system we could possibly employ. You all have an equal chance.

LADY. Step aside please, Miss.

MRS HENDRY, *the Matron of the Hospital enters and sees the* BOYS *spying on them.*

MRS HENDRY. Aaron! Toby! Get away from there at once! You know you shouldn't be there.

TOBY *and* AARON. Sorry, Mrs Hendry. Sorry, Ma'am.

They run off.

Scene Two

TOBY *and* AARON *come charging outside into the fresh air.*

TOBY. If I'm a black ball and you're a white ball, where are all the red balls?

AARON *laughs.*

AARON. Mish can be a red ball. He's a carrot-top.

TOBY. Yes! Mish is a red ball.

A group of girls suddenly runs up and surrounds AARON. *They begin chanting:*

GIRLS.
Quick, quick, say your prayers,
Blow out the candle and climb the stairs,
Who will come to kiss you goodnight,
Close your eyes and shut them tight,

In and out and round and round,
Lie down, stay on the ground,
In and out and round and round,
She's creeping up without a sound,
It could be her, it could be me,
But which one will it be,
In and out and round and round,
Don't move, stay on the ground,
In and out and round and round,
Open your eyes 'cause you've been found!

*AARON is kissed by a cheeky girl – MOLLY JENKINS.
TOBY laughs his head off.*

AARON. Get off, Molly Jenkins.

The GIRLS laugh and run off.

TOBY. She loves you. She wants your babies.

AARON. No one wants babies!

*MRS HENDRY appears. She rings a bell. Lots of
CHILDREN run up and form two lines – BOYS on one side
and GIRLS on the other. TOBY and AARON join their
line.*

MRS HENDRY.
John, Peter – stables!
Jane, Constance – dairy!
Stephen, Joseph – wood-shed!
Mary, Charlotte – wash-room!
Alfred, Samuel – cow-shed!
Anne, Molly – kitchens!

Aaron, Toby . . .

TOBY *and* AARON (*quietly*). Garden. Garden. Garden . . .

MRS HENDRY. Garden!

TOBY *and* AARON. Yes!

They tear off to the gardens.

TOBY. Let's find him!

AARON. Mish! Mish!

*They spot MISH standing like a scarecrow in the vegetable
garden, waving his arms to shoo away the birds. It is
MESHAK GARDINER, so much healthier and happier
looking that he is almost unrecognisable.*

TOBY. There!

AARON. Mish!

They rush to him and fling their arms around him. He is thrilled to see them and picks them up and spins them round.

MISH. Angel child! Tobykins!

AARON. Was I a white ball or a red ball, Mish?

MISH. No balls in the vegetables. Not allowed.

AARON. No. When you brought me here?

TOBY. I didn't need a ball because I was special. My mother was a princess in Africa. And we'll go and find her and she'll look after all of us.

AARON. On a big ship.

TOBY *and* MISH. Across the dark ocean.

AARON. Was I a white ball, Mish, when you brought me here?

MISH (*confused*). No balls. They were kind to Mish and his Angel child.

TOBY. He means they didn't have the balls then. They just let anyone in.

AARON. That's why they let you in.

TOBY growls and tries to squash AARON's head.

TOBY (*to* MISH). Are you his Da?

MISH. Yes.

TOBY. Are you his Ma?

MISH. Yes. Mish Da and Mish Ma.

The BOYS laugh. AARON hugs him.

AARON. You're so funny, Mish.

MISH. Apples today.

AARON. Be my horse.

TOBY. Be my horse. It's my turn.

MISH picks both of them up and carries them off.

Scene Three

The Chapel at the Foundling Hospital. The organ is being played. AARON *creeps in – drawn by the wonderful, thrilling music. He sees the organist – a broad-backed man, hunched over his instrument. Every so often he breaks off and scribbles something on a piece of paper, muttering to himself. This organist, unknown to* AARON, *is* GEORGE FRIDERIC HANDEL. AARON *creeps further forward and finds a hiding place to listen from. The music holds and transports him.*

A CLEANER *enters with a bucket, making an enormous clatter.* HANDEL *stops playing immediately and turns on him.*

HANDEL. Du lieber Gott.

CLEANER. Sorry, Sir. I was told the rehearsal was finished, Sir.

HANDEL. Quiet with you!

The CLEANER *hurries out, but in his irritation,* HANDEL *has dropped several pages of his manuscript which flutter down to the floor.*

Mein Gott!

AARON *scurries from his hiding place and collects them up. He takes them to* HANDEL *and gives them to him.*

Thank you, my boy.

AARON. You're welcome, Sir.

AARON *turns to go.*

HANDEL. Wait. What are you doing here, creeping around like a little mouse, eh?

AARON. Sorry. Sorry, Sir. I heard the music and I wanted to see.

HANDEL. You like music?

AARON. Yes, Sir. I love music.

HANDEL. Can you play?

AARON. No, Sir.

HANDEL. Sing you in the choir?

AARON. No, Sir. I'm not old enough yet, Sir.

HANDEL *suddenly stands and picks* AARON *up. He stands him on the organ stool.*

HANDEL. Sing me something.

AARON (*alarmed*). Sing?

HANDEL. Go on. Sing!

AARON *sings 'He Shall Feed His Flock'. He sings it perfectly. His voice is clear and strong and passionate. When he has finished,* HANDEL *stares at him for some time.*

HANDEL. How do you know this music?

AARON. I've heard it here, Sir. When I'm in the schoolroom I can hear them practising – the choir and all the musicians.

HANDEL. Do you know what this music is?

AARON. I know it's for a concert. To raise money for us. We're orphans.

HANDEL. This music is mine. It is called *Messiah*.

AARON. Really? It's the best music I've ever heard.

HANDEL. I should think it is.

HANDEL *stares at him.*

You have the gift.

AARON (*confused*). We aren't allowed gifts.

HANDEL. You have the gift of music. The greatest gift. See –

He makes AARON *look closely at his eyes.*

You have made me weep. What is your name?

AARON. Aaron. Aaron Dangerfield. Mr Dangerfield is my benefactor. I'll be apprenticed to him.

HANDEL. What to do?

AARON. Cabinet-maker, Sir.

HANDEL. Nein, nein, nein. This cannot be so. I will talk to your choirmaster about you – your Mr . . .

AARON. Ledbury, Sir.

HANDEL. Yes. I will talk to him about you.

A bell sounds in the yard.

Yes. Run along now.

AARON *gets down and starts to go.*

AARON. Goodbye, Sir.

HANDEL. I will talk to him. Aaron Dangerfield.

Scene Four

MRS HENDRY *is in her office. A* MAID *enters, leading* TOBY *and* AARON *in. They look sheepish.*

MAID. The boys you wanted, Mrs Hendry.

MRS HENDRY. Thank you.

The MAID *leaves.*

Aaron. Toby. Do you know why you are here?

TOBY. Is it because of the mud pie?

MRS HENDRY. No. No it isn't. Though you can tell me about that later if you would like.

TOBY. No thanks, Ma'am.

MRS HENDRY. Boys, I have asked you here to tell you that your time with us is at an end. On Friday you will both be leaving to begin new lives. Toby, you will go to join the household of your benefactor, Mr Gaddarn, as a liveried servant. You will be housed and fed. You will be allowed to attend church on Sundays and have one day off a year. Mr Gaddarn is a good and important man. He gives a great deal of money to support our work. I trust you will serve him well.

TOBY. Yes, Ma'am.

MRS HENDRY. Aaron. You are not yet eight and normally a little young to be apprenticed out. But Mr Handel believes you have superior talents in music. We have spoken with Mr Dangerfield and he has kindly agreed that you may now be apprenticed to a musician named Mr Brook, a protegee of Mr Handel. You will be instructed in the art of music copying and you will also be given musical tuition.

AARON. Music! I really want to do music!

MRS HENDRY. Now, as you are probably aware, it is our practice when a boy leaves to give him back any token which he came here with. Many of you had mothers who loved you very dearly and wished you to have something to remember them by.

She picks up a colourful string of beads from a tray on her desk.

Toby, this string of beads was around your neck when you were brought here.

TOBY *takes it. He is amazed and overwhelmed. His mother must have held this, touched it.*

TOBY. Do you know where my mother is?

MRS HENDRY. No, I'm afraid I don't. The stranger who brought you here said he found you in Bristol. It is most likely that your mother was a slave, en route to the Indies.

TOBY. But she's a princess. And she's free now.

MRS HENDRY *only smiles.*

MRS HENDRY. Aaron . . . I'm afraid we have nothing for you. There was nothing with you when you came.

AARON *is deeply disappointed. He fights back tears.*

As you know, it was Mish who brought you here. He was in a very sorry state himself and we could ascertain nothing about where he found you. I'm sorry.

TOBY. But you've got Mish. He's like your token.

MRS HENDRY. Quite right. And that's more than many have.

AARON. Yes.

MRS HENDRY. So, on Friday a carriage will be sent to collect you, Toby; and Aaron, Mr Ledbury himself will accompany you to Mr Brook's.

AARON. Does Mish know I'm going?

MRS HENDRY. Yes. I explained to him this morning.

AARON. Will he come with me?

MRS HENDRY. Mish will be allowed to stay on here. He works very hard and it has always been felt that he would not survive outside the hospital. Go forth bravely, boys. Be a credit to Mr Coram and to all of us.

Scene Five

TOBY *and* AARON *run outside.*

TOBY. I'm going in a carriage!

AARON. I'm going to learn music!

TOBY. I'm going to be liveried!

AARON. Liveried means covered in liver.

TOBY. No it does not!

They fight and tumble together. Then they stop and are quiet for a moment.

AARON. Can I see the necklace?

TOBY *takes it carefully from his pocket and lets him take it for a moment.*

TOBY. Don't break it.

AARON. Do you think she made it?

TOBY. Course she did.

AARON. I like the colours.

TOBY *takes it back.* AARON *watches him staring at it and feeling the beads between his fingers.*

We will still be friends, won't we?

TOBY. Course. We'll always be friends.

AARON *goes to find* MISH *in the garden. He is suddenly feeling very sad.* MISH *stops what he is doing and hugs him tightly.* AARON *starts to cry.*

MISH. Angel child has to go. I know. Angel child will be happy.

AARON. I'll come back and see you all the time. And when I'm grown up, I'll sing and make lots of money and I'll come and get you, and you and me and Toby will go and find his mother.

MISH. On a big ship.

AARON. Across the dark ocean.

They hug some more. MISH *dries* AARON's *eyes.*

Mish . . . I know you're my Ma and my Da, but did I ever have a real mother? Like Toby? I mean, a lady?

MISH *looks away and shakes his head.*

Try to remember. Please. Did you ever see her? A lady? Did she speak to you? Was she beautiful?

MISH. Mish Da, Mish Ma.

AARON *nods, resignedly.*

AARON. I love you, Mish.

MISH. I love you, Angel child. My Angel child.

[handwritten margin note: Mish (Meshak) keeps the secret of Aaron's birth]

Scene Six

AARON *is waiting nervously in a pleasant room with* MR THOMAS LEDBURY, *the Coram choirmaster.* THOMAS *looks out of a window.*

THOMAS. Well, this isn't a bad old place, eh? Good view of St Martin's Lane.

AARON. Yes, Sir. Have you met Mr Brook, Sir?

THOMAS. No. I understand he hasn't been in England for long. But Mr Handel thinks a lot of him. Bit nervous, are you?

AARON *nods.*

First time out of the hospital. It's bound to seem strange. Where was your friend off to in that carriage?

AARON. A house by the river. Near Billingsgate. Mr Gaddarn's.

THOMAS. Well, that's not too far, eh? Think of it as moving up in the world. I remember when I first went to stay in a smart house – a huge place, much bigger than this. I kept thinking I was going to get lost, or walk into someone else's room by mistake.

AARON *smiles.* THOMAS *takes a paper bag of toffees from his pocket.*

Do you want a toffee?

AARON *(excited).* Thank you, Sir.

THOMAS. Oh – perhaps you'd better not eat it now if you're going to sing. Put it in your pocket for later. In fact, take the lot.

AARON (*taking them*). Thanks, Mr Ledbury.

THOMAS. Never know when you'll need the toffee cure. Why don't I sing you a funny song? Eh? While we're waiting. Take your mind off things.

AARON. Yes, please.

THOMAS. Just don't tell Mrs Hendry when you see her.

THOMAS *crosses to a harpsichord and opens the lid.*

Now then – (*Beginning to play and sing.*) In Gloucester Docks, so I . . . (*Stopping.*) Perhaps not.

He sings a funny version of the Coram Hymn. AARON giggles. ALEXANDER enters quietly and stands in the doorway, watching. A smile breaks through his habitually sad expression.

ALEXANDER. I thought I told you not to sing those songs, Thomas.

THOMAS *looks round in astonishment. He rises to his feet.*

THOMAS. Alex? Alex!

He flies at ALEXANDER and they hug.

Alex. But . . . Edward Brook! Why didn't I think of it? Did you know it was me? I mean, did you . . .

ALEXANDER. I hoped it was you, when Mr Handel mentioned your name.

THOMAS. This is wonderful. This is the best. Aaron. Sorry. This is Mr . . . ?

ALEXANDER. Brook.

THOMAS. Brook. Mr Brook. We knew each other when we were boys.

ALEXANDER. Hello, Aaron.

ALEXANDER *offers his hand to AARON. He takes it and shakes it sombrely.*

AARON. Hello, Sir.

ALEXANDER. You're very welcome here. I'm looking forward to working with you.

THOMAS. Perhaps we should . . . ?

ALEXANDER. Yes.

THOMAS. Aaron, will you sing for Mr Brook now?

ALEXANDER. Yes. Let me hear this voice I've heard so much about. And then you can go and get settled in. You must be tired.

AARON. Thank you, Sir.

THOMAS *sits at the harpsichord again. He begins to play* ALEXANDER*'s song – 'I Will Praise Thee'.* ALEXANDER*'s eyes fill with tears.* AARON *finishes.* THOMAS *looks at* ALEXANDER *and smiles kindly.*

THOMAS. You know me – I only have to hear something once.

Scene Seven

At MR GADDARN*'s house,* TOBY *is being dressed in his 'livery'. It is the costume of an exotic African prince, with satin pantaloons and a richly embroidered jacket. On his feet he wears gorgeous, jewelled slippers which turn up at the ends, and on his head is placed a silk turban with a huge shining glass ruby in the centre of it. Finally, a silver tray is placed upon his upturned hand.* TOBY *is in awe of this splendid costume.*

A man enters. He is wearing a powdered wig and clothes of the finest quality. This is MR PHILIP GADDARN.

GADDARN. Well. Let's have a look at you.

He looks TOBY *over and smiles.*

Good. Very good. Do you know who I am?

TOBY. Mr Gaddarn, Sir. I'm very grateful to you, Sir.

GADDARN. And what do they call you?

TOBY. Toby. Toby Gaddarn, Sir.

GADDARN. Toby Gaddarn. My own little foundling boy. And what do you think of your costume? Quite the little prince, eh?

TOBY. I love it, Sir. I love this big jewel.

Pause. MR GADDARN *is just staring at* TOBY.

GADDARN. So you think you'll be happy here?

TOBY. Oh yes, Sir.

GADDARN. Why aren't you smiling then?

TOBY *immediately smiles.*

Is that the biggest smile you've got?

TOBY *smiles more broadly.*

Wider.

TOBY *forces his mouth into an exaggerated smile.*

That's how wide I expect your smile to be, every time I look at you.

TOBY. Yes, Sir.

GADDARN. People like your smile. They like your pink tongue. They like how black your skin is from your head to your toes.

He gets very close to TOBY, *who keeps trying to smile.*

You serve my guests. You get them anything they want, give them anything they want. You never say no, and you never, ever tell a soul about anything you see in this house. Is that understood?

TOBY. Yes, Sir.

GADDARN. Do you know what I do to telltales? I cut out their tongues and nail them to their bedposts as a reminder of what they shouldn't have done. I'd hate to do that to you – seeing as how your tongue is so pink. Now get out there and serve. And smile, Toby Gaddarn.

Scene Eight

In ALEXANDER*'s house,* ALEXANDER *and* THOMAS *are having a drink together.*

ALEXANDER. Are you in touch with them?

THOMAS. The occasional letter from Isobel. They're all fine and well – as far as I know.

ALEXANDER. Good. That's very good.

THOMAS. You've had no contact at all?

ALEXANDER. None. Melissa – is she still with them?

THOMAS. I believe so. Yes – Isobel mentioned that she and her mother are running an orphanage now, on the estate.

ALEXANDER *nods. This is affecting him very deeply.*

And I hear Edward is at Eton. Alex, I'm assuming you don't know this . . .

ALEXANDER. What? What?

THOMAS. Your father . . . he disinherited you.

Pause.

ALEXANDER. Oh. Well, it was the sensible thing to do.

THOMAS. I'm glad you can see it that way.

ALEXANDER. I thought you were going to say something really awful.

THOMAS. Like what?

Pause.

ALEXANDER. I don't even know. It's been difficult . . .

THOMAS. Of course.

ALEXANDER. Knowing they were all there. That she was there. Thomas . . .

THOMAS. Your mother was distraught when you left. They did search for you, you know?

ALEXANDER. Yes.

THOMAS. Where did you go?

ALEXANDER. Switzerland. For a while. Lied about my age and got a job as a music tutor. Then I made my way to Germany . . .

THOMAS. On the trail of Mr Handel.

ALEXANDER. Yes. And that led me back here to London. I'd made some good contacts in Leipzig. They'd given me letters of introduction.

THOMAS. And now you're working with him. It's really extraordinary. When I think how you idolised him.

ALEXANDER. The man's a genius. And he's been very kind to me.

THOMAS. And your music? You must have written some wonderful stuff.

ALEXANDER. What about you? Let me guess – you're married with three children.

THOMAS. Not yet. But there's plenty of time for that.

ALEXANDER. And the Coram choir – that's really something.

THOMAS. I love it.

ALEXANDER. You deserve to be happy, Thomas.

THOMAS. So do you.

ALEXANDER. I don't know . . . I don't know if I understand happiness.

THOMAS. Of course you do.

ALEXANDER. Even Mr Handel has noticed it. In my music. 'It's good, Alexander, very clever – but where is the joy?' That song of mine – just listening to it then – it's the best thing I've ever written.

THOMAS *is shocked and unsure whether he is serious.*

I used to write for God. Everything was very clear. But since I left . . . (*He trails off.*)

THOMAS. But your gift is still there. Of course it is.

ALEXANDER. No. The colours don't come.

Pause.

I think I need to go back.

Scene Nine

In the drawing room at MR GADDARN's *house.* AARON *and five other* BOYS *are singing 'He Shall Feed His Flock'.* HANDEL *is accompanying them on a harpsichord.* ALEXANDER *is turning the pages for him.* THOMAS *is conducting the* BOYS.

There is an audience of wealthy-looking PEOPLE. *To one side,* TOBY *is standing, dressed in his livery, trying to smile. At the back, looking on, is* MR GADDARN. *The piece comes to an end. The* AUDIENCE *applaud.* HANDEL *takes a bow.* MR GADDARN *comes forward.*

GADDARN. I would like to begin by thanking Mr Handel for choosing to hold this – the first of what he terms his 'rehearsals' – in my humble abode. As you are probably all aware, the music these fine little fellows have sung for us today is by way of an appetiser for the performance of Mr Handel's masterwork . . .

HANDEL. *Messiah.*

There is a ripple of applause.

GADDARN. *Messiah* which is to take place at the Coram Hospital on Christmas Eve. And I'm sure you all agree, if this 'rehearsal' is anything to go by, then we are in for a rare and sumptuous treat. Mr Handel is a fellow benefactor of the Coram Hospital. All the money raised from that performance will be donated to Coram funds – a very generous gesture, if I might say. And what better cause could there be? Every time I look at my own little Coram boy, here . . . (*He indicates* TOBY.) my heart swells with pride. The way a nation treats its poor and unfortunate citizens, most especially its children, is a mark of how civilised it truly is. And I say, looking about me this afternoon, England is civilised indeed!

Everyone applauds.

Now please feel free to linger for a while, and enjoy a little of my simple hospitality.

The AUDIENCE *stand and disperse. Many gather around* HANDEL *to congratulate him. Some talk to the* BOYS, *some to* THOMAS. MR GADDARN *passes close to* ALEXANDER *and bows as* ALEXANDER *moves aside.* ALEXANDER *stares after him as though he recognises him.* AARON *goes straight to* TOBY, *who has begun serving delicacies from his silver tray.*

AARON. Tobes! You look splendid. And look at this place. It's like a palace!

TOBY. Why haven't you been to visit me?

AARON. Sorry. We've been rehearsing for the concert all the time. And when they said we were coming here, I thought it would be a good surprise for you.

TOBY. I don't like surprises any more.

He walks away.

AARON. Toby?

TOBY. I'm not allowed to speak to people.

THOMAS *manages to free himself from appreciative* PEOPLE *and hurries towards* ALEXANDER.

THOMAS. Alexan . . . Edward!

ALEXANDER. Aaron sang beautifully.

THOMAS. He did. Listen . . .

ALEXANDER. His voice inspires me. I mean, it actually makes me feel that I have to write.

THOMAS. I knew you two would be good for each other. But listen. I've had a letter from Isobel. She is absolutely overjoyed to know that you're back. She sent this note for you.

He hands the note to ALEXANDER.

ALEXANDER. Thank you.

THOMAS. And there's more. I asked if she would approach your parents about the idea of me taking the boys to sing at Ashbrook. A small concert like this. And your mother has said yes.

ALEXANDER. Yes? Really?

THOMAS. Really. She's organising it all. Inviting wealthy people from the district.

ALEXANDER. This is wonderful. But what about my father? Has he agreed too?

THOMAS. She didn't say. But this is the beginning, Alex. They're allowing music back – they're allowing me back! Surely it can only mean they want you back too?

In a quiet corner of the room, AARON *catches up with* TOBY.

AARON. Don't walk off. What's wrong?

TOBY. As if you care.

AARON. I'm sorry I didn't come before. You could have come and seen me, you know.

TOBY. I'm not allowed out.

AARON. Look.

He takes the bag of toffees out of his pocket and offers them to TOBY.

Mr Ledbury gave me them. I saved half for you.

TOBY (*taking them*). Thanks.

He turns away and starts to cry.

AARON. Tobes? Are you crying?

TOBY. No.

AARON. What's wrong? Aren't you happy here? Tobes?

TOBY. I hate it.

AARON. But why? It's amazing.

TOBY. You don't know what it's like.

AARON. Look . . . why don't we go to your room and you can tell . . .

TOBY. I haven't got a room.

AARON. Where do you sleep? (TOBY *doesn't reply.*) Toby.

TOBY. Can we go and find my mother?

AARON. What?

TOBY. I want to go soon. Tomorrow or the day after.

AARON. Tobes, I can't. We're going to all these big houses to sing. And it's the concert in a few weeks. And I like it at Mr Brook's. He's kind and he never shouts and I love the music.

TOBY. Just go away.

AARON. If you're not happy you should tell Mr Gaddarn.

TOBY. He's horrible. He's going to cut my tongue out.

AARON. Cut your tongue out? Don't be silly.

TOBY. You don't believe me!

AARON. I . . .

TOBY. I'm going to find my mother. Soon! And you're not coming. She's my mother anyway!

He walks out of the room. Sadly, AARON *goes back to join the other* CORAM BOYS.

Scene Ten

TOBY *enters a dark room. It is wood-panelled, with long leaded windows that look out over the docks. There is the shadowy outline of maps on the walls, and books on high shelves. He crosses to a large globe which stands in the corner of the room. He squats down next to it and turns it until he finds Africa.*

TOBY. Africa.

> *With his finger, he traces a line from Africa to the New World.*

> Virginia.

> *He takes his mother's beads out of his pocket and rubs them between his fingers.*

> I'm coming soon. I'm coming soon.

> *He curls up on the floor next to the map and sobs.*

> *Back in the drawing room, left alone with the harpsichord,* ALEXANDER *tentatively begins to play. In his mind's eye, he sees* MELISSA, *glowing like an angel.*

Scene Eleven

A few hours later. It is dark outside. TOBY *has fallen asleep.* PEOPLE *are approaching the door.* TOBY *wakes with a start as he hears* MR GADDARN'*s laugh. Horrified, he looks about and spots a silk screen at the other side of the room. He darts behind it, just in time. The room lights up with dancing shadows, as* MR GADDARN *enters carrying a candelabra which he sets down on a table. There are two other* MEN *with him. They all sit down, and* MR GADDARN *pours drinks from a decanter.*

GADDARN. I can get four boys and three girls by the end of the month.

MAN 1. Only three girls? Six would make it far more worth our while. Yours too.

GADDARN. The Coram authorities keep records. Details. For every child I take possession of, I have to produce written

evidence of where they're going, which family they're going
to, their terms of labour. I have contacts who forge documents
for me, but it takes time and there's no room for mistakes.
Doing it for three girls is possible, six isn't.

MAN 2. I have a contact in the North Country who could do
the same thing for you. The Coram people aren't likely to
go checking up there.

GADDARN. I only use my own people.

MAN 2. He's good. I'll vouch for him.

Pause. MR GADDARN *thinks for a few moments.*

GADDARN. Where would the girls be going?

MAN 1. Turkey. Some would go on to North Africa. We'd
keep the best ones for the harems in Istanbul.

GADDARN. Which trader do you use?

MAN 1. Abdul Fazir. We've used him every time.

Pause.

GADDARN. I'll try for six.

MAN 1. Good.

GADDARN. At two hundred apiece.

MAN 2. Two hundred? You're not serious?

MAN 1. That's twice the going rate.

GADDARN. I thought you came to me because you wanted
Coram girls. That's what they cost. They aren't just scum
you pick up off the streets. They're educated, free of disease
and they're pure as the day they were born. I'll guarantee
them, every one. But if it's too much for you, gentlemen,
there's plenty of other people I can do business with.

The two MEN *look at each other.*

MAN 1. Two hundred apiece then. But if any of them prove to
be unsound in mind or body, we get our money back.

GADDARN. If a single one proves unsound, you'll get all
your money back. But if I decide, even at the last moment
that six is too many and it has to be three, then three it will
be. Agreed?

MEN. Agreed.

GADDARN. I will not risk my reputation with Coram. It's cost me too much. Now – I think this calls for a drink, don't you?

They knock their glasses together and drink.

MAN 2. How do you do it, Gaddarn? How do you get them onto the ships without anyone noticing?

MAN 1. I've often wondered that.

MAN 2. And where do you keep them – until the ships are in?

GADDARN. Trade secret, gentlemen. Let's just say . . . let's just say, I move heaven and earth. (*He stands.*) Shall we?

They leave the room. After a few moments, TOBY *comes out from his hiding place. He is trembling and horrified by what he has heard. He hurries from the room.*

Scene Twelve

TOBY *enters the drawing room. It is very different now from how it was at the concert. It is littered with* PEOPLE *in masks and elaborate wigs and ostentatious clothes. Some of the* WOMEN *are so revealingly dressed as to suggest they might be prostitutes. Everywhere,* PEOPLE *are drinking and smoking, gambling and groping.* MR GADDARN *is circulating, always watching. A* SERVANT *approaches him and offers him a drink but he declines.*

A LADY *sees* TOBY *and calls to him.*

LADY. There you are! Where have you been, my little prince? Come here at once.

He goes to her and she pulls him down onto her knee.

Mm. Gorgeous. Utterly gorgeous. Feel his hair.

Another LADY *does so and giggles.*

Could you ever imagine a human being so black? Show them your tongue, little monkeykins.

TOBY *sticks out his tongue. The* LADIES *shriek.*

LADY 2. Good heavens!

LADY 3. I wonder what will happen to him when he's too big to sit on our laps.

LADY. He'll never be too big to sit on mine!

They shriek with laughter.

What are you going to do when you're a lovely big man? Are you going to come and live with me? How much would you want for him, Philip?

MR GADDARN *approaches.*

TOBY. I'm going to find my mother.

LADY. Oh. And where is she?

TOBY. The New World. (*Holding up his beads.*) She gave me these.

LADY 3. Go near the New World and they'll make a slave of you.

TOBY. My mother's not a slave. She's free and she's a princess.

GADDARN. Who told you that? Your mother's a slave. That's if she's not dead. Don't start getting ideas. As far as you're concerned, this is as good as it gets.

TOBY *feels utterly crushed.*

Scene Thirteen

THOMAS, AARON *and five other* CORAM BOYS *have arrived outside Ashbrook House. They are full of excitement and gaze at the house with awe.* MISH *is with them. He has paused in his task of unloading their luggage and is staring at the house. A terrible feeling is creeping through him – a realisation that he has been here before and that bad things happened when he was here.*

BOY 1 (*pointing*). That's my room!

BOY 2. I'm getting a whole wing!

AARON *goes to* MISH.

AARON. It's enormous, isn't it? What's wrong?

MISH. Not here.

AARON. But this is Ashbrook House. This is where we're singing.

MISH. Ashbrook.

AARON. Yes.

MISH. I'm not happy.

AARON. But why? We'll have a wonderful time.

MISH. I'm not happy here.

MISH *runs off towards the stables.*

AARON. Mish! Mish!

THOMAS. Come on, now, boys – help with the boxes!

ISOBEL *comes rushing from the house, shortly followed by* MELISSA.

ISOBEL. Thomas!

THOMAS. Isobel.

They go to greet each other – but there is a slight moment of embarrassment when they don't know whether it's all right to hug or kiss. In the end, THOMAS *kisses* ISOBEL's *hand.*

And Melissa.

He does the same to MELISSA *who is smiling at him warmly.*

My goodness! Two beautiful ladies – how on earth did that happen?

They laugh. ALICE *comes running up. She is almost exactly the same age as* ISOBEL *was.*

And don't tell me this is Alice?

ALICE. Of course it's me.

THOMAS. Three beautiful young ladies! I don't know what I shall do.

LADY ASHBROOK *approaches.*

LADY ASHBROOK. Thomas. It's a pleasure to see you again.

THOMAS. It's a pleasure to be here, Lady Ashbrook.

LADY ASHBROOK. I think I would have recognised you immediately. The same sunny smile.

She is smiling, but there is a great deal of emotion in her voice.

THOMAS. Thank you for having the boys here.

LADY ASHBROOK. I couldn't be more delighted. I have long
been an admirer of the Coram Hospital. We have emulated
the Coram methods in our orphanage here at Ashbrook.
Now, I thought you could perform in the drawing room.

THOMAS. Wherever you want us.

LADY ASHBROOK. I've brought in an instrument for you –
a harpsichord.

THOMAS. Thank you.

MRS LYNCH *has come outside.*

LADY ASHBROOK. Let's get all these little chaps settled in,
shall we? Boys! Boys! Follow Mrs Lynch, please.

The BOYS *run inside.* LADY ASHBROOK, ALICE *and*
MELISSA *go too.* ISOBEL *can't wait to speak to*
THOMAS.

ISOBEL. How is he?

THOMAS. He's well. He's in Gloucester. He thought he
should wait there until we know how things stand.

ISOBEL. Gloucester! So close. I can hardly bear it.

THOMAS. He just wants to come home. Do you think it's
possible?

ISOBEL. I don't know. It all depends on Papa.

THOMAS. Is he here?

ISOBEL. He'll be back this evening. Thomas, he doesn't know
about the concert.

THOMAS. I see.

ISOBEL. Mama decided not to tell him. I think . . . There's
been such an awful silence these last eight years, such a
terrible strain . . .

THOMAS. Yes.

ISOBEL. I know it puts you in a difficult position. Mama does
too. If you want to turn around and go back . . .

THOMAS. No. I wouldn't dream of it.

ISOBEL. Oh, Thomas. Should we tell her about Alex? If
there's going to be trouble, perhaps it's better that we tell
her now.

THOMAS. Let's hold our nerve. See what happens tonight.

MELISSA *comes back outside.*

MELISSA. Lady Ashbrook is asking where you want everything.

THOMAS. Right. Thank you.

MELISSA. Is Alexander all right?

ISOBEL. Yes. Why don't you write to him? Thomas could deliver the letter.

MELISSA. No. I have no call on his heart.

ISOBEL. But . . .

MELISSA. People change. We were practically children.

ISOBEL. But . . . you'll tell him about the baby?

MELISSA. I don't know. I don't know if I want to. I don't think it would be fair. I manage. I've managed for all these years.

ISOBEL. You must tell him. I'm sure he would want to know.

MELISSA. It would have been his birthday today – our little Alex.

ISOBEL. Oh, Melissa! Oh, that's terrible. How could I have forgotten?

MELISSA. It's all right.

ISOBEL. It must have been because of Thomas coming and . . . I'm awful.

MELISSA. It's all right. Darling, Isobel. No one could have been a more constant friend than you.

Scene Fourteen

In the drawing room, everything is being put in place for the concert. MELISSA and MRS MILCOTE have brought in drinks and cake for the BOYS, who are eating happily. THOMAS is supervising. MRS MILCOTE, who looks rather ill and worn, passes close to THOMAS.

MELISSA. Mother, you remember Thomas?

MRS MILCOTE. Oh. Yes. Yes. How do you do?

THOMAS. Well. Thank you.

    MRS MILCOTE *moves away.*

MELISSA. I'm afraid she hasn't been in good health for some time.

THOMAS. I'm very sorry to hear that.

    Pause.

MELISSA. The children are adorable.

THOMAS. Yes. Most of the time.

MELISSA. I look at the children in the orphanage sometimes and I marvel at them; at their enthusiasm, their resilience, their hope. There is so much we can learn from them.

    Outside, MISH *has come to peer in through the window in search of* AARON. *He sees* MELISSA *and the shock has a physical effect on him. He turns away.*

THOMAS. One of these boys is apprenticed to Alexander.

MELISSA. To Alex? Which one?

THOMAS (*pointing to* AARON). That one.

MELISSA. I knew you would say that one.

THOMAS. Aaron? Come here, please.

    AARON *comes to them – wondering what he's done wrong. But* MELISSA *smiles warmly at him. Outside,* MISH *looks through the window again. He sees* MELISSA *and* AARON *together.*

MELISSA. Hello, Aaron.

AARON. Hello, Miss.

MELISSA. Have you had a cake?

AARON. Yes, thank you, Miss.

MELISSA. Well, you must have another. And how old are you, Aaron?

AARON. I'll be eight next week, Miss.

MELISSA. Will you really? Eight. That's a lovely age.

MISH *watches as she smooths* AARON's *hair and straightens his collar.* MISH *rushes away to a quiet corner, panicking and distressed.* For the first time in eight years he feels the need to be dead. *He lies down on the ground and his eyes roll back into his head. But terrible memories flood back to him, of* OTIS's *harsh voice and mothers wailing and babies crying.*

MISH. Angel? Angel!

His ANGEL *is suddenly there – but as he rushes towards her he suddenly stops. She is not smiling – she looks angry.*

ANGEL. Tell him, Meshak.

MISH. No!

ANGEL. Tell him. Give him his mother. Give me my son.

MISH. No! No!

He wakes himself up. He sits up and cries.

You leave him! My Angel child. Mish Da. Mish Ma.

Scene Fifteen

That evening, in the drawing room, the CORAM BOYS *give their concert.* THOMAS *accompanies them on the harpsichord. All the* ASHBROOK FAMILY, *with the exception of* SIR WILLIAM *are there, along with several* NEIGHBOURS *and local* DIGNITARIES. ISOBEL *throws anxious looks towards the door, watching for her father.* LADY ASHBROOK *maintains complete composure.*

The moment comes for AARON's *solo – 'Oh Death, Where Is Thy Sting'. He stands and begins to sing. His voice is strikingly like* ALEXANDER's *at the same age. What is more, he even looks like* ALEXANDER – *particularly when he sings. All the* FAMILY *notice it. It is almost too much for* LADY ASHBROOK. *And* MELISSA *and* ISOBEL *find their minds full of thoughts of what might have been. But it is particularly shocking to* MRS MILCOTE. *She rises from her chair for a moment, hardly able to breathe.* MELISSA *looks at her in concern and draws her back down. But she continues to stare and to tremble.*

At this moment, SIR WILLIAM *enters. He can hardly believe what he is seeing or hearing. But he is overwhelmed – at the sound of that voice.* LADY ASHBROOK *and* ISOBEL *glance at him. It is impossible to know what he is thinking.*

Just before the music finishes, SIR WILLIAM *strides from the room.* LADY ASHBROOK *sees him go.* ISOBEL *and* THOMAS *exchange a significant look.*

When the concert ends, the AUDIENCE *applaud warmly.* LADY ASHBROOK *holds herself together to thank the* BOYS. MRS MILCOTE *sees* MRS LYNCH *and catches her arm.*

MRS MILCOTE. Did you hear him? The boy?

> MRS LYNCH *draws* MRS MILCOTE *to one side.* MELISSA *glances round and watches with concern.*

Are you certain he is dead? Are you quite certain? He is so like Alexander.

> *The name seems to reverberate around the room.* PEOPLE *turn and look at them.*

MRS LYNCH (*whispering*). Do you or do you not pay me for my silence?

MRS MILCOTE. Yes. But . . .

MRS LYNCH. Then let us *be* silent.

> MRS LYNCH *walks away.* LADY ASHBROOK *walks from the room.*

Scene Sixteen

LADY ASHBROOK *rushes to find* SIR WILLIAM. *He is standing in the hallway.*

LADY ASHBROOK. William?

SIR WILLIAM. How did this happen? Why did you allow this?

LADY ASHBROOK. Because I've seen you. I've seen you in church when the choir is singing. Look at you. Your eyes have filled with tears now because of that boy's voice.

SIR WILLIAM. I feel it! Yes. I feel it. But that does not mean that I regret what I did. It does not mean that I relent or that my position has changed in the slightest way.

LADY ASHBROOK. But why? Why? Why must we go on suffering like this? Nothing is worth this. I cannot bear it any longer! I'm sorry, but I cannot bear it. I cannot bear it.

She begins to cry, desperately. SIR WILLIAM *goes to her and holds her. Behind them,* THOMAS *and* ISOBEL *enter.*

Scene Seventeen

In her bedroom, MRS MILCOTE *is clutching the pink shawl which she found in the wood.*

MRS MILCOTE. Dear God. Dear God, can it be true?

Scene Eighteen

At MR GADDARN's *house,* TOBY *is looking out of a window onto the street. He looks hollow-eyed and desperate. The* PARLOURMAID *sees him and shouts at him:*

MAID. Get on with that polishing I gave you. What d'you keep looking at, anyway?

TOBY. I'm looking for my friend. I sent him a note.

MAID. He'll have forgotten all about you. Now go and get on with it.

TOBY *starts to go back to the kitchen. But as he comes into the hallway he sees a line of* GIRLS *approaching. They are being led by two of* MR GADDARN's *SERVANTS. They are* CORAM GIRLS, *and there are six of them.* TOBY *is immediately alarmed. He pulls back so as not to be seen. The* GIRLS *pass by. He recognises one as* MOLLY JENKINS. *She is smiling and excited.*

TOBY. Molly!

MOLLY. Oh, no. Toby Gaddarn. You look awful! I'm going to a big house in the country.

TOBY. No, Molly . . .

MOLLY. Out of my way, slave!

The SERVANT *leads the* GIRLS *into the map room.* TOBY *follows at a distance. Inside the room,* MR GADDARN *is waiting.* TOBY *peers round the door, shaking with fear. He is holding his mother's beads in his hand, worrying them between his fingers.*

GADDARN. Now, girls, let me show you to some temporary accommodation. It's just for a day or two.

He moves the big globe. A panel slides open in the wall behind it, revealing the dark entrance to a passageway. TOBY*'s eyes grow wide.*

One of the SERVANTS *steps into it.*

Follow the man.

The GIRLS *look suddenly fearful.*

MOLLY. In there? But it's dark. And it's wet.

GADDARN. There's lights further down the passage. Don't you worry now. Go on.

MOLLY *reluctantly goes in, followed by the other* GIRLS. TOBY *hears them call out:*

MOLLY. I don't like it in here!

GIRL. Can we go back?

MR GADDARN *turns away and says to the other* SERVANT.

GADDARN. Close it up when he's out. Feed 'em twice a day.

MR GADDARN *suddenly heads towards the door.* TOBY *starts and rushes away, but in his panic he drops his mother's beads.* MR GADDARN, *hearing footsteps, is instantly suspicious. He sees the beads and picks them up. A terrible look appears on his face.*

Toby Gaddarn.

He goes off to find him.

Scene Nineteen

*The following day, in the drawing room at Ashbrook.
ALEXANDER is standing alone by the harpsichord. He
begins to play – a new piece of music he is writing. Suddenly
ALICE appears. She stops short when she sees him.
ALEXANDER stops playing.*

ALICE. Are you him?

    ALEXANDER *stares at her.*

ALEXANDER. Alice?

ALICE. Are you him? Are you . . .

SIR WILLIAM. Alexander.

    ALEXANDER *looks up.* SIR WILLIAM *has entered
behind* ALICE.

Yes, Alice. This is Alexander.

*Father and son look at each other for several moments, then
walk towards each other and embrace.*

*LADY ASHBROOK and ISOBEL then come hurrying in
and throw their arms around him. They are followed by
MRS MILCOTE and MELISSA. THOMAS stands in the
doorway, beaming. MELISSA hangs back as EVERYONE
surrounds ALEXANDER.*

*At the window, MISH appears. He sees ALEXANDER and
watches as ALEXANDER's eyes meet MELISSA's for the
first time. His fear of losing AARON intensifies.*

*MELISSA holds ALEXANDER's gaze for several
moments, but then she leaves the room and the house. MRS
MILCOTE has been watching her and follows her outside.*

MRS MILCOTE. Melissa? Where are you going?

MELISSA. I can't . . . I'm sorry.

*She walks off in the direction of Waterside. MRS MILCOTE
pursues her.*

MRS MILCOTE. At least come back into the house! Melissa!

*But MELISSA disappears into the woods. MRS MILCOTE
turns to go back. MISH, who has followed MELISSA's
movements, is caught unawares and finds himself face to*

face with MRS MILCOTE. *They both freeze, and both are instantly taken back to the night of the baby's birth.*

You!

MISH *starts to run.*

Wait! Wait! The baby! What happened to the baby? Please . . .

Scene Twenty

At Waterside, MELISSA *is sitting amongst the disused dolls and cradles. The door opens and* ALEXANDER *walks in. They look at each other for some time before either can speak.*

ALEXANDER. Isobel told me you would be here. I should have known it anyway.

MELISSA. I'm very glad you've come home.

Pause.

ALEXANDER. You look well. Exactly as I remember you.

MELISSA. I don't think that can be true.

Pause.

ALEXANDER. Melissa . . . I thought of you. Every day. I want you to know that there was never anyone else . . . anyone who . . .

MELISSA. Alex . . .

ALEXANDER. I am not naive as I was then. I know I have no right to expect anything. But if there remains the slightest affection for me . . . in your heart . . . I left my heart with you. Nothing has really touched me since . . . I am asking for a chance . . . a chance to . . .

MELISSA. Stop, Alexander, please.

ALEXANDER. You don't care for me. Of course.

MELISSA. It's not . . .

ALEXANDER. Is there someone else? Forgive me, I have no right to . . .

MELISSA. Yes.

ALEXANDER *is astonished. It is like a physical blow to him.*

No! That's not what I mean. Alex . . . after you left . . .
We had a child. There was a baby. Stillborn. A boy.

Pause.

ALEXANDER. We had a child.

MELISSA. He was . . . stillborn. I'm sorry.

At this moment, ISOBEL *is heard calling as she runs
towards the cottage.*

ISOBEL. Melissa! Melissa!

She bursts through the door.

Your mother. She's collapsed. Come quickly.

Scene Twenty-One

Evening. MRS MILCOTE *is lying in bed. She has not awoken
since she collapsed.* MELISSA *is sitting beside her, watching
and worrying. Suddenly,* MRS MILCOTE *stirs.*

MRS MILCOTE. Melissa?

MELISSA. Mother. Mother. Thank God. Here.

*She puts a glass of water to her mother's lips and she
drinks a little.*

MRS MILCOTE. Did they stop him?

MELISSA. Who?

MRS MILCOTE. Did they catch him?

MELISSA. Who? Mother, I don't know what you mean.

MRS MILCOTE. You have to find him. You have to bring him
to me.

MELISSA. Who? Don't worry about anything now.

MRS MILCOTE. Meshak. His name was Meshak Gardiner.

MELISSA. Gardiner?

MRS MILCOTE. The son. The son.

MELISSA. You mean the son of that man who hanged? The
murderer?

MRS MILCOTE. Oh, my Lord. My Lord.

MELISSA. Please don't get upset, Mother. The doctor said . . .

MRS MILCOTE. Is she listening?

MELISSA. Who? Do you mean Mrs Lynch?

MRS MILCOTE. She mustn't hear. She mustn't know I have
told you.

MELISSA. She's not here, I swear it. Mother, has Mrs Lynch
been . . . has she been demanding money from you because
of . . . ?

MRS MILCOTE. Oh, my darling. Oh, my girl. My girl.

MELISSA. Why didn't you tell me? I have wanted to ask you
so many times, but you made it so plain that you never
wanted me to mention him.

MRS MILCOTE. Oh, my darling . . .

MELISSA. I thought you must be disgusted with me.

MRS MILCOTE. Never. Never that. But you must listen to me
now. Listen. There is another secret which she keeps. A
secret which has eaten away at my soul so that I can hardly
live.

MELISSA. What? You're frightening me.

MRS MILCOTE. You cannot forgive me, but please try to
understand. I only ever did what I thought was right for
you. Melissa, your baby . . . he was not stillborn. He was
not dead. I held him and I felt his heart beating.

MELISSA *is silent.*

He was alive. He was alive when we gave him to Otis
Gardiner.

MELISSA*'s blood runs cold.*

MELISSA. Otis Gardiner?

MRS MILCOTE. He was meant to take him to the Coram
Hospital. But then we found the bodies in the woods . . .

MELISSA. Oh, no . . .

MRS MILCOTE. I found my shawl – the shawl we wrapped
your baby in. I found it.

MELISSA. No.

MRS MILCOTE. But Melissa, listen to me . . .

MELISSA. No. Oh, no.

MRS MILCOTE. The boy – the Coram boy – he is so like you. He is so like Alexander. And Meshak Gardiner was there. Do you see? That night. I saw him. And now he has come here with the boy.

MELISSA. What are you saying?

MRS MILCOTE. What if he took him? What if he saved your baby and took him to the Coram Hospital?

Scene Twenty-Two

In the kitchen, the CORAM BOYS, *with the exception of* AARON, *are just sitting down to eat.* THOMAS *is supervising.* MELISSA *comes rushing in. She scans the* BOYS' *faces.*

THOMAS. Hello. How is she?

MELISSA. Where's Aaron?

THOMAS. Aaron. Yes. I was just thinking that myself. He's normally first at the table.

MELISSA. Where is he?

THOMAS. Boys, do you know where Aaron is? (*They take no notice.*) Boys! Do any of you know where Aaron is?

BOY. He went off with Mish.

MELISSA. Mish?

THOMAS. Dear oh dear. When did they go?

BOY. Ages ago.

MELISSA. Who's Mish? Who's Mish?!

THOMAS. Aaron's friend. Red-haired fellow. He came along to ride shot and help with the horses.

MELISSA *has turned white.*

MELISSA. Meshak.

THOMAS. Are you all right, Melissa?

ALEXANDER *enters.*

ALEXANDER. Melissa? What's happening?

She looks at him.

MELISSA. Aaron. It's Aaron.

Scene Twenty-Three

In the drawing room at Ashbrook. SIR WILLIAM, LADY
ASHBROOK, ISOBEL, MELISSA, ALEXANDER *and*
THOMAS *are all sitting around a table.* ISOBEL *is holding*
MELISSA*'s hand.* ALEXANDER *sits silently, trying to make
sense of everything that has happened.*

SIR WILLIAM. I have men combing every inch of the
countryside. And I have sent word to the Coram Hospital.

THOMAS. I doubt he would take him back there. Not if he
doesn't want to be found.

LADY ASHBROOK. Where else might he go?

THOMAS. He must know Gloucestershire like the back of his
hand.

ISOBEL. At least we know that this Meshak cares for Aaron.

There is a knock at the door and MRS LYNCH *enters. She
looks momentarily shocked when she sees the whole family
confronting her, but she immediately recovers her composure.*

MRS LYNCH. You wanted to see me, My Lady?

They are all staring at her with dislike and anger.

LADY ASHBROOK. Mrs Lynch . . .

SIR WILLIAM. Do you know anything at all about what
happened to my grandson?

LADY ASHBROOK (*to* SIR WILLIAM). Wait. Please. Mrs
Lynch, Melissa and Isobel have told Sir William and I about
the baby. They have also told us about your part in what
happened that night.

Pause.

MRS LYNCH. Her mother and I agreed it was for the best.

LADY ASHBROOK. To tell a girl that her baby is dead when
it is not?

MRS LYNCH. What else could we do? What could she have
    done with it? Would you have been happy if she had
    brought it to you? No. You would have told them both to
    leave and hoped you would never see them again.

LADY ASHBROOK. That is simply not true.

SIR WILLIAM. Do not be insolent, woman.

MRS LYNCH. And if you hadn't sent them away, he would
    have done. (*She indicates* SIR WILLIAM.) A man who
    would disown his own son.

The ASHBROOKS *are utterly shocked.* LADY ASHBROOK
is moved to defend SIR WILLIAM.

LADY ASHBROOK. How dare you speak to Sir William in
    such a way?

MRS LYNCH. People like you do not forgive these things.
    I should know. You are very selective in your compassion.
    You show a sort of sweeping mercy to those so far beneath
    you they don't matter, but when it comes to anything which
    might threaten your perfect world, then, then the iron gates
    come down. And love counts for nothing. I gave her baby to
    the Coram Man because I believed he would take it where
    it would be cared for . . .

SIR WILLIAM. You really expect us to believe that?

MRS LYNCH. I had no idea what he did with those babies.

SIR WILLIAM. You were lying then and you're lying now.
    What else do you know about that night? What do you
    know about this boy Meshak?

MRS LYNCH (*categorically*). I know nothing.

LADY ASHBROOK. I will try very hard to believe you, Mrs
    Lynch. Until today you have never given me cause to doubt
    your word. But for you to demand money from Mrs Milcote
    in return for your silence, poor Mrs Milcote who must have
    been suffering unbearably, that is beyond forgiveness. To
    make money from the suffering of others takes a
    particularly nasty human being. And I can no longer have
    you in my employ.

MRS LYNCH. I have no wish to remain in this house. As for
    making money from the suffering of others, I think you will
    find it is something we all do . . .

SIR WILLIAM. Get out!

MRS LYNCH. The silk on your back, the sugar in your tea, all of this – all wealth is built upon the suffering of others.

SIR WILLIAM. My wife is the most charitable woman in this county. Her orphanage is an example to every parish for . . .

MRS LYNCH. She could fund five orphanages if she chose to sell one ring on her finger.

SIR WILLIAM. Get out of my house!

MRS LYNCH. You people disgust me. I hope you will be called to account one day.

She starts to go.

ALEXANDER. Philip Gaddarn. Does the name mean anything to you?

She freezes in her tracks.

MRS LYNCH. No, it does not.

He scrutinises her face. She holds his gaze. Then she leaves the room. There is silence for a moment. Her accusations and manner have stunned them.

THOMAS. Why did you ask about Gaddarn?

ALEXANDER. Because that day at the concert . . . at Gaddarn's house. I felt quite certain I'd seen him before. And now I know who he is: Otis Gardiner.

SIR WILLIAM. Otis Gardiner hanged. On the gibbet at Stroud. I saw it myself.

ALEXANDER. And yet there is a man living in London, a benefactor of the Coram Hospital, who I would swear is him. Who oversaw the hanging?

SIR WILLIAM. Claymore – the magistrate.

ALEXANDER. Could we speak to him?

LADY ASHBROOK. He has moved away.

ISOBEL. There was an awful business with his ward – she took her own life.

Pause. MELISSA *begins to cry, silently.*

LADY ASHBROOK. But if this man is Otis Gardiner . . . you don't think Meshak would take the boy there?

SIR WILLIAM. He can't be Otis Gardiner, I tell you.

Pause.

THOMAS. What do we do?

ALEXANDER. I think we should go to London and talk to Mr Gaddarn. Whoever he is, or was, at this moment he's all we've got.

ALEXANDER *approaches* MELISSA *and kneels down beside her.*

I'll find him. I'll find our son.

She looks at him but cannot reach out to him.

Scene Twenty-Four

MISH *is walking through countryside with* AARON. *Over his shoulder,* MISH *has a shotgun.* MISH *suddenly stops and points.*

MISH. Look!

AARON *looks. It is London – spread out before them.*

AARON. London! It's London.

He jumps down and hugs MISH.

Oh, Mish, you *are* taking me home. Thank you. Thank you.

MISH. We're not going home.

AARON. I mean, to Mr Brook's.

MISH. No.

AARON. Or we can go to the hospital if you like. And Mr Ledbury could take me back. And we could ask about you coming too.

MISH. Angel child and Mish are finding Toby.

AARON. Toby?

MISH. We'll go on the big ship with Toby.

AARON. No. Mish, no. I don't want to go on a ship. I don't think it would work, looking for Toby's mother. He doesn't even know where she is.

MISH. Big ship. Across the dark ocean.

AARON. No, Mish. I don't want to. I want to go back to Mr Brook's.

MISH. No!

AARON. I want to do the singing. I'm going to miss the concert!

MISH suddenly grabs him hard and shakes him.

MISH. Angel child stays with Mish.

AARON. I will stay with you, but we have to go back.

MISH. Mish Ma, Mish Da.

AARON. You're hurting me!

MISH. They'll take you away. They'll beat Mish. They'll hurt Mish. Bad Mish. Bad, bad.

AARON. No, Mish. It'll be all right if you take me back. You're hurting me!

MISH suddenly needs to be dead. He collapses down onto the ground and his hands twitch and his eyes roll back.

Mish! Mish! Don't! What are you doing? Mish! I'll stay with you. I will. We'll go and get Toby. Don't, Mish. Don't.

Scene Twenty-Five

Evening. MRS LYNCH is waiting in the map room. A SERVANT enters, closely followed by MR GADDARN: OTIS GARDINER. On seeing MRS LYNCH, OTIS stops in his tracks.

OTIS. Well, well. Mrs Lynch.

MRS LYNCH (*indicating the* SERVANT). Tell him to go.

OTIS. There's no need.

He is staring at her, scrutinising her. The difference in their stations is very apparent.

I knew I'd see you again – one way or another.

MRS LYNCH. They're onto you.

OTIS. Who are?

MRS LYNCH. The Ashbrooks.

OTIS. The Ashbrooks?

MRS LYNCH. They asked me about Philip Gaddarn. I mean it. They know.

OTIS (*to* SERVANT). Put a watch on the doors – front and back. If anyone comes near this house, you tell me.

The SERVANT *nods and leaves.*

How could the Ashbrooks know? I haven't been near Gloucester.

MRS LYNCH. The son has been in London. He's seen you. And Meshak is back.

OTIS. Meshak?

MRS LYNCH. Yes. Meshak! He's taken a boy. A boy they think is their grandson. It could be their grandson. The Ashbrook baby. Do you remember? The night that Meshak disappeared?

OTIS. Jesus Christ! Jesus Christ!

MRS LYNCH. You have to get out.

OTIS. No!

MRS LYNCH. Yes, Otis! This is it. They are onto you. They won't let this go.

OTIS. What can they prove? People saw me hang. What are they going to do? Dig up the body of that other poor beggar? A body eight years old!

MRS LYNCH. Half of this game is knowing when to quit and move on.

OTIS. I'm not leaving all this! Look at it! Don't you pretend you're not impressed!

MRS LYNCH. I can't help you – not this time!

The SERVANT *suddenly appears.*

OTIS. What?

SERVANT. They were at the back door, Sir.

MISH *and* AARON *step anxiously into the room.* MISH/ MESHAK *sees* OTIS *and his heart almost stops beating.*

AARON. Sorry, Sir. We didn't mean to be any trouble. We just wanted to see Toby.

OTIS. Hello, Meshak.

MESHAK suddenly bolts for the door, but the SERVANT grabs him and slams him against a wall.

AARON. Mish! Get off him! Help! Toby! Help! Toby . . . !

OTIS grabs AARON under his arm and stifles his mouth. MESHAK is still struggling.

MESHAK. No!

The SERVANT has grabbed the shotgun off him and he now hits him in the face with it.

OTIS. You just couldn't do it, could you? You couldn't crawl into a ditch and die?

Outside the room, TOBY has heard AARON's cry and has started to head towards it. He is covered in cuts and bruises. There is blood all down his shirt and whip marks on his back. He peers around the door and sees AARON and MESHAK, captives.

(*To SERVANT.*) Open the passage. We'll take them straight out there.

MRS LYNCH. Think what you're doing. Think now, Otis.

OTIS. They couldn't have timed it better. The ship's sailing tonight.

MRS LYNCH. What ship?

The SERVANT pushes the globe and the entrance to the passageway opens. From in the passageway the GIRLS' voices start up:

GIRLS. Let us out! Help us, please!

OTIS watches the amazed look on MRS LYNCH's face and grins.

OTIS. Welcome to my world.

The SERVANT and OTIS pull MESHAK and AARON into the passage. MRS LYNCH follows. She covers her nose and mouth to keep out the smell. They pass the CORAM GIRLS, dirty and pale with terror. They reach out to them. Some of them wail louder when they recognise MESHAK and AARON. MRS LYNCH pauses and stares at them.

Scene Twenty-Six

Out on the street, ALEXANDER *and* THOMAS *are just approaching* MR GADDARN's *house.*

THOMAS. This is the one.

TOBY comes hurtling out of the front door of the house. There is a SERVANT there who grabs him.

SERVANT. No you don't.

But TOBY *bites him hard and the* SERVANT *lets go of him, shrieking with pain.* TOBY *reaches the street and looks this way and that, panicking, not sure where to go, but knowing he must tell someone. He is about to run off, when* THOMAS *calls to him:*

THOMAS. Toby!

TOBY looks round, terrified. But when he sees THOMAS he runs towards him.

Toby? My God, what's happened to you?

TOBY. He's got them. Aaron and Mish.

ALEXANDER. Gaddarn?

TOBY nods and tries to catch his breath.

THOMAS. Come on.

They are about to head into the house but TOBY stops them.

TOBY. No! I know where he's taking them. To the docks. Through the passage. I know where it comes out.

THOMAS. Show us.

Scene Twenty-Seven

At the docks. OTIS, MRS LYNCH, *the* SERVANT, MESHAK *and* AARON *are just emerging at the end of the tunnel from the house. Ahead of them now, they can see the River Thames and a ship moored very close by.*

But suddenly, ALEXANDER, THOMAS *and* TOBY *come running up. They stop when they see the extreme danger of the*

situation. The SERVANT *still has the shotgun. And*
ALEXANDER *is shocked to see* MRS LYNCH. *But the sight
of his son being roughly held, and his terrified face, make*
ALEXANDER *recklessly brave.*

ALEXANDER. That boy is my son. Let him go.

OTIS. You just back off, Mister.

THOMAS. We know who you are, Gaddarn.

ALEXANDER. Let him go! You won't escape. Let them both
go. I'll speak for you. I'll save you from the gallows.

OTIS. I'm going nowhere near the gallows.

ALEXANDER (*approaching steadily*). Aaron, I'm your father.
Don't be afraid. It will be all right . . .

ALEXANDER *suddenly makes a grab for* AARON. *The*
SERVANT *raises the gun but* MESHAK *begins to struggle
like an angry bull and it is all he can do to control him.*
ALEXANDER *and* OTIS *are locked in a struggle.*
ALEXANDER *manages to push him aside and is about to
take hold of* AARON *when* OTIS *pulls a knife.*

THOMAS. Alexander!

ALEXANDER *looks round in time to see the blade coming
at him.* THOMAS *throws himself in front of* ALEXANDER
and takes the blow. He falls to the ground.

ALEXANDER. Thomas . . . Thomas!

A blow comes down on ALEXANDER*'s head. He falls and
hits his head on the stone ground. He is unconscious.*

AARON. No!

The SERVANT *from the front of the house runs up.*

OTIS. Get them on the ship. I'll go back for the girls.

The SERVANTS *lead* MESHAK *and the* BOYS *away.*
OTIS *turns to pick up the gun, but* MRS LYNCH *grabs it
first. She turns it on him.*

What's this?

MRS LYNCH. Leave the girls.

He goes to walk past her. She pulls the trigger back.

OTIS. What's the matter with you? Do you know how much
they're worth? They'll set us up again.

MRS LYNCH *says nothing.*

For God's sake! Surely you knew? Where do you think all this came from? (*He indicates his fine clothes.*) Bit late to find your conscience, ain't it?

MRS LYNCH. You have five seconds to get onto that ship before I scream for help. One . . .

OTIS. You're mad! Do you want to get caught?

MRS LYNCH. I never get caught. Two. Three. Four . . . I'm sorry, Otis. Five. (*Shouting.*) Help! Help here! I need help! Help!

OTIS. You mad bitch. I hope you rot in hell.

He runs off to the ship. She stops shouting and watches him go. ALEXANDER *begins to stir.* MRS LYNCH *walks off, in the opposite direction from the ship.*

Scene Twenty-Eight

MESHAK, AARON *and* TOBY *have been locked in a hold on the ship.*

AARON. We're in the hold!

TOBY. What are we going to do?

AARON. We're moving. We're moving!

TOBY. No!

AARON (*to* MESHAK). Why did you have to take me away? Mr Brook said he's my father! Why did you take me?

MESHAK (*crying*). Sorry. Sorry.

AARON. It's all your fault. All of it! All of it!

MESHAK *suddenly realises what he has done. He goes to the wooden door of the hold and throws himself against it, pushing with all his might.*

Go on, Mish, you can do it! Go on!

TOBY. Push, Mish!

The door gives way.

AARON. Come on!

They climb out.

Scene Twenty-Nine

On the deck, OTIS *turns and sees them come out and rush towards the ship's rails.*

OTIS. Fancy a swim, do you?

AARON (*dismayed*). We're too far out. I can't do it.

TOBY. We've got to. I won't be a slave. I can't be a slave, Aaron.

OTIS laughs.

AARON (*unsure what to do*). Mish?

TOBY climbs up on the rail.

Toby, no!

OTIS (*walking towards him*). Don't want to be a slave, eh? Go on then. What's stopping you?

He grabs hold of TOBY *and throws him over the side.*

AARON. Toby . . .

AARON climbs the rail and jumps over too.

MESHAK. No!

He rushes at OTIS *and hurls him to the ground. The two of them struggle.* MESHAK *gets his hands round* OTIS's *neck.* OTIS *draws his knife and stabs* MESHAK *in the stomach.* MESHAK *feels suddenly weak.* OTIS *scrambles away from him and looks aghast when he sees the blood pouring from him.* MESHAK *looks up at him.*

Da?

OTIS cannot speak.

Da?

He staggers to his feet and lurches to the rails, where AARON *and* TOBY *went in.*

OTIS. Don't, Meshak! Don't be a fool!

But MESHAK *throws himself overboard. On the deck,* OTIS *sinks to his knees. He feels utterly wretched and sick.*

In the water, MESHAK, AARON *and* TOBY *are fighting for their lives. None of them can swim.* MESHAK, *though badly injured, desperately tries to push the* BOYS *upwards to the surface.*

The water begins to whisper MESHAK's *name. A strange light begins to shine around him. With one last, enormous effort he pushes the* BOYS *up. He lets go of* TOBY *and then* AARON.

MESHAK. Angel . . .

And the BOYS *are gone, and his* ANGEL *is there in front of him. She smiles and opens her arms.*

ANGEL. Come now, Meshak. Come to me.

The light grows. She swoops down over him and he feels the absolute joy of her embrace.

Scene Thirty

Christmas Eve. In the chapel at the Coram Hospital, the CHOIR *are taking their places to sing* Messiah. HANDEL *is sitting at the organ.*

SIR WILLIAM *and* LADY ASHBROOK *are sitting on the front row of the packed and excited* AUDIENCE. MRS MILCOTE *is sitting beside them, followed by* ALICE. ISOBEL *is sitting with* THOMAS, *whose arm and chest are bandaged as a result of his wound. They are all dressed in black and all look sad and strained.* MELISSA *keeps looking round anxiously.*

HANDEL. Where is our conductor, eh? Mr Brook?

The BOYS *look around for him.*

The *Messiah* cannot wait. It is almost Christmas!

Some of the AUDIENCE *laugh, but the* ASHBROOKS *look at each other with concern.* MELISSA *stands.*

MELISSA. Excuse me.

She walks towards the door of the chapel. Then she spots ALEXANDER. *He is sitting alone in a secluded corner. She goes to him.*

Alex?

He looks up at her.

ALEXANDER. I can't do it.

She sits down next to him.

I keep picturing Meshak's body . . . the way it looked
when they pulled him from the water. And then I think of
Aaron . . . and I wonder if . . . somewhere . . .

MELISSA. Don't.

ALEXANDER. And Toby. It could all have been so different.

Pause.

MELISSA. We have to try. We have to try to find a way to live.

ALEXANDER. Why did this happen? Was it our fault?

MELISSA. No.

ALEXANDER. Did we do something so very wrong?

MELISSA. No. We did nothing wrong. I loved you, Alex. I love
you still.

*He looks at her and they embrace. Holding each other
desperately.*

Everyone's waiting.

ALEXANDER *nods. They start to walk towards the*
CHOIR. MRS HENDRY *hurries up behind them.*

MRS HENDRY. Mr Brook? There are two boys at the door –
late arrivals – they want to know if they can still join in.

ALEXANDER. I'm afraid not. I think we must begin now . . .

MELISSA. Alex . . .

He turns and follows her gaze. Slowly, from out of the light,
AARON *and* TOBY *come walking towards them, hand in
hand. They look dishevelled and tired but otherwise no
worse for wear. They reach them.* ALEXANDER *takes*
AARON's *hands, as if he might not be real.*

ALEXANDER. Aaron, Aaron.

The ASHBROOKS *and* THOMAS *slowly stand, unable to
believe what they are seeing.*

AARON. Is it true, Sir? Are you my father?

ALEXANDER. Yes. Yes, I am.

AARON. But what about Mish?

ALEXANDER. Mish . . . was your father too. But he's with
the angels now. He'll be your guardian angel. Always. Do
you understand?

AARON. I think so.

MELISSA. Hello, Aaron.

ALEXANDER. This . . . Aaron, this beautiful lady is your
mother.

AARON *looks at* MELISSA.

AARON. But I haven't got a mother, Sir.

MELISSA. Yes you have. Yes you have. You both have.

MELISSA *and* ALEXANDER *put their arms around*
AARON *and* TOBY *and hold them tight.*

HANDEL. Mr Brook! You choose a very inconvenient time to
discover your joy.

AARON. Could you let go of me now, please? I'm sorry, but I
really have to sing.

ALEXANDER. Go, Aaron. Go and sing.

AARON *goes and takes his place in the* CORAM CHOIR.
ALEXANDER *hugs* MELISSA *one last time before leaving
her with* TOBY *and going to conduct* Messiah – *with great,
great, joy.*

End.

MUSIC

The Gloucester Clipper

Lyrics by Helen Edmundson
Music by Adrian Sutton and Helen Edmundson

Voice

At Glouces-ter docks, so I___ heard tell, where fi-sher wives ga-ther, their catches to sell, The

Violin
(F-C-G-D)

rar___ est ves-sel you e - ver did see, Cries Who will come fish-ing, come fish-ing with me?

CHORUS O - ver and un - der and haul him to sea,

Who will come fish-ing, come fish-ing with me?

I'm a fast-going clipper, kind fellows, cried she
I'm ready for cargo, my hold it is free
Come give me a rope now and take me in tow,
From yardarm to yardarm a-towing we'll go

chorus

Billy stepped up he was ready to go,
He clambered aboard and she took him below,
He lifted her hatches, found plenty of space,
But his jib-boom was bent and he sank without trace

chorus

Johnny was desperate and up for the chase,
He drew alongside at a hell of a pace,
Her foresails were lowered, her staysails undone
But his shot-locker emptied before he'd begun

chorus

Her eye fell on Thomas, so handsome and fine,
Her prow rose to meet him, she threw him a line,
He filled her with fishes, she begged him for more
And he never let up 'til he'd run her ashore

chorus

Here's luck to the girl with the curly black locks,
Here's luck to the girl who ran Bill on the rocks,
Here's luck to the girl who led Johnny astray,
Raise a cheer now for Thomas who showed her the way

chorus

Alex's Anthem – 'I Will Praise Thee'

Music by Adrian Sutton

Three Children Sliding

Lyrics by John Gay
Music by Adrian Sutton

Alice

Three chil - dren sli - ding on the ice, U - pon a sum - mer's day It
(Now) had these chil - dren been at home, Or sli - ding on dry ground, ten
par - ents all that chil - dren have, and you that have got none, If

Edward

Three chil - dren sli - ding on the ice, U - pon a sum - mer's day It
(Now) had these chil - dren been at home, Or sli - ding on dry ground, ten
par - ents all that chil - dren have, and you that have got none, If

so fell out they all fell in, The rest they ran a - way, The rest they ran, the
thou-sand pounds to one pen ny They had not all been drowned, They had not all, they
you would keep them safe a - broad, Pray keep them safe at home, Pray keep them safe, pray

so fell out they all fell in, The rest they ran a - way, The rest they
thou-sand pounds to one pen ny They had not all been drowned, They had not
you would keep them safe a - broad, Pray keep them safe at home, Pray keep them

The Coram Hymn

Music by Adrian Sutton
Lyrics Anonymous